NUT MILKS
AND NUT BUTTERS

NUT MILKS
AND NUT BUTTERS

- Simple ways to make great-tasting nut and seed products at home
- Boost your health, and nourish your body
- Replace dairy with nature's blockbuster nutrients

Catherine Atkinson

LORENZ BOOKS

This edition is published by Lorenz Books,
an imprint of Anness Publishing Ltd,
108 Great Russell Street,
London WC1B 3NA;
info@anness.com

www.lorenzbooks.com; www.annesspublishing.com;
twitter: @Anness_Books

If you like the images in this book and would
like to investigate using them for publishing,
promotions or advertising, please visit our website
www.practicalpictures.com for more information.

Publisher: Joanna Lorenz
Senior Editor and Designer: Lucy Doncaster
Special photography: Debby Lewis-Harrison
Food stylist for special photography: Stephanie
   Knowles-Dellner
Production Controller: Rosanna Anness

PUBLISHER'S NOTE
Although the advice and information in this book
are believed to be accurate and true at the time of
going to press, neither the authors nor the publisher
can accept any legal responsibility or liability for any
errors or omissions that may have been made nor for any
inaccuracies nor for any loss, harm or injury that comes
about from following instructions or advice in this book.

ACKNOWLEDGEMENTS
The author and publisher would like to thank
Vitamix for the loan of a machine for the testing
and development of the recipes in this book.
www.vitamix.co.uk. They would also like to thank
Lakeland for the loan of a Vitamix blender for use during
the photography shoot. For hundreds of electrical food
prep items, and lots more visit www.Lakeland.co.uk

NOTES
• Bracketed terms throughout the book are
intended for American readers.
• For all recipes, quantities are given in metric
and imperial measures and, where appropriate,
in standard cups and spoons. Follow one set
of measures, not a mixture, because they are
not interchangeable.
• Standard spoon and cup measures should
be level. 1 tsp = 5ml, 1 tbsp = 15ml, 1 cup =
250ml/8fl oz.
• Australian standard tablespoons are 20ml.
Australian readers should use 3 tsp in place of
1 tbsp for measuring small quantities.
• American pints are 16fl oz/2 cups. American
readers should use 20fl oz/2.5 cups in place of
1 pint when measuring liquids.
• Electric oven temperatures in this book are for
conventional ovens. When using a fan oven, the
temperature will probably need to be reduced by
about 10–20°C/20–40°F. Since ovens vary, you
should check the manufacturer's instruction book
for guidance.
• The nutritional analysis given for each recipe,
unless otherwise stated, is calculated per portion
(i.e. serving or item). If the recipe gives a range,
such as Serves 4–6, then the nutritional analysis will
be for the smaller size, i.e. 6 servings. The analysis
does not include optional ingredients, such as salt
added to taste.
• Medium (US large) eggs are used unless
otherwise stated in the recipe.

SAFETY NOTE
Any food has the potential to cause an allergic
reaction, but peanuts, as well as walnuts, Brazil
nuts, hazelnuts, almonds and sesame seeds are
known to be common allergens. In cases of
extreme allergy, nuts can trigger a life-threatening
reaction known as anaphylaxis. Symptoms include
facial swelling, shortness of breath and loss of
consciousness, so it is essential that sufferers take
every precaution to avoid nuts.

CONTENTS

Nut and seed milks and butters 6
Nuts for health 8
All kinds of nuts   10
All kinds of seeds   16
Tools and equipment   18
Making nut milks 20
Making seed and grain milks 30
Making coconut milk and coconut
    products 32
Blending, flavouring and using milks 34
Making nut butters 40
Making seed butters 48
Using nut and seed butters 50

Recipes using nut and seed
    milks and butters 52

Breakfasts and drinks 54

Soups 64

Snacks and salads 72

Main courses 84

Desserts 104

Baking 116

Index 126
Additional nutritional information 128

NUT AND SEED MILKS AND BUTTERS

From the simple diet of the earliest hunter-gatherers to the lavish banquets enjoyed by the Greeks and Romans, nuts have long been a valued food. In modern times, they are still a major part of the diet of the rainforest tribes of South America and a staple for many West African and Asian people, yet in the Western world the greatest sales of nuts are as highly salted snack foods, often roasted in saturated or hydrogenated fats. This is a pity, as nuts in their unadulterated state have much to offer. Protein-rich and packed with vitamins and minerals, they can improve immunity and help protect against disease. Although they have a relatively high fat content, this is mostly heart-healthy monounsaturated and polyunsaturated fats and, together with a high plant sterol content, these can help lower cholesterol levels.

In the last few years, as many people have recognized the nutritional attributes of nuts, demand for healthy nut products have increased and supermarkets have started to stock nut milks alongside dairy milk, as well as a wide range of nut and seed butters. A decade ago, almond milk was the only nut milk you could buy, and it could only be found in a small number of health-food stores. Now it is widely available, along with hazelnut and coconut-based milks. Nut butters have followed the same pattern: once only peanut butter could be found on supermarket shelves; now there is a wide range of types including hazelnut, almond, cashew, pumpkin and sunflower seed butters.

A brief history
While almond and other nut milks and the variety of nut butters may be new to modern-day supermarkets, nut milks and nut butters have been around for centuries. Almond milk has always been a feature of Middle-Eastern cuisine and was also enjoyed by prosperous families in Europe during the Middle Ages when almonds were an expensive and highly desirable import. At that time, without modern refrigeration, dairy milk did not stay fresh for long, and although it could be purchased daily from street vendors, it was often contaminated, diluted with water, or on warmer days would sour within hours. Instead, the rich relied on nut milk made from either almonds or walnuts. Making the milk was labour-intensive, as the nuts had to be pounded by hand with a pestle and mortar, but the creamy liquid could be stored for several days. As a bonus, it could be drunk on the many days when the church placed restrictions on the consumption of dairy products.

◀ Nut milks and butters are easy to make at home and make nutritious dairy-free inclusions in everyday recipes.

▲ **Above left** Wholesome and delicious, nuts are as versatile as they are diverse. **Above right** There are many different types of commercially-made nut and seed milks available, but it is easy to make your own.

It was around this time that 'blancmanger' was enjoyed, a white-coloured dish set with gelatine in a fancy mould. It was made with chopped chicken breast braised in almond milk, and sweetened with honey. This has been modified, leaving out the chicken, into the still-popular nursery dessert blancmange.

Of all nut butters, peanut butter is the most famous. The Aztecs were probably among the first people known to make a crushed oily paste from peanuts, and the Incas used peanuts as offerings to the Gods and entombed them with their mummies as early as 1500BC. Early travellers took groundnut (peanut) plants to Africa and eventually they spread in the same way to other parts of the world. Fast-forward several thousand years to Canadian Marcellus Gilmore Edson, who was the first person to patent peanut butter in 1884. His product, which sold at 6 cents per lb, was a peanut purée with a solid consistency like chilled butter. It was developed as a nutritious food for people who no longer had all their teeth and were unable to chew, which was not uncommon at that time. Almost a decade later, Dr. John Harvey Kellogg created a creamier version in which the peanuts were steam-cooked rather than roasted, and this high-nutrient food was served to patients at his health sanatorium. It was not a great success and the Kellogg brothers moved to other products and eventually became famous for their breakfast cereals.

Commercial production of peanut butter began in 1908, but early products had a gritty texture, a short shelf-life and were inconsistent. Gradually, a method of preventing the oil from separating, advanced machinery and roasting the nuts to improve their flavour resulted in a creamy texture and its popularity rapidly grew.

Making your own nut milks and butters
Whether you make nut products or buy store-bought ones is up to you. Commercially-made nut milks and butters can be used in all the recipes in this book, but check cartons and jars carefully; ideally you should select unsweetened nut milks with a high nut content and butters made without hydrogenated oil stabilizers, or large amounts of sugar or salt. Making your own is as simple as blending soaked nuts in water to make nut milks, or grinding nuts to a paste for nut butters, with or without flavourings. The results are fresh and delicious products that can be more economical than ready-prepared ones. You can also tailor them to exactly suit your own preferences.

NUTS FOR HEALTH

Nuts are nutritional powerhouses. Packed with protein, vitamins and minerals, and heart-healthy omega-3 fats, they make a great contribution to a balanced diet. Fresh nuts have been eaten and used in cooking for centuries, yet in the last two decades most of those sold in large supermarkets and smaller retailers are packets of nuts that have been roasted in oil and heavily seasoned to create high-fat, high-salt unhealthy snacks. Although sales for these hasn't declined, consumer demand for unsalted nuts, nut and seed milks and a range of nut butters has recently seen a rapid increase.

NUTS FOR DIFFERENT LIFESTYLES

Nuts can be eaten by those who need or choose to follow restricted diets, including vegetarian and vegan, dairy-free, paleo, low-sodium, low-carbohydrate and high-fibre regimes.

Vegetarian Nuts contribute a good level of protein as well as minerals such as iron and zinc, which can be lacking in a meat-free diet. They contain between 10–25 per cent protein and many, such as peanuts and almonds, have as much as the same weight of cheese. While no single nut contains all nine essential amino acids (the building blocks of protein), this can easily be remedied by eating foods with complementary amino acids – ie by eating chickpeas on the same day as almonds.

Dairy-free Nut milks are particularly useful for those who are lactose or dairy intolerant as they can be used to replace dairy milk in most recipes; they can also be made into yogurt for eating or for use in cooking. Nuts are an excellent source of calcium, which is usually supplied by dairy food in the diet.

▲ Nuts have many nutritional and health benefits and are suitable for most types of diet.

Paleo The paleolithic diet is based on food eaten during the paleolithic era on the basis that our body's nutritional needs evolved at that time. It excludes dairy products, grains, legumes, processed oils and refined sugars. All nuts and seeds are suitable for the paleo diet with the exception of peanuts, which are legumes.

Low-sodium Nuts and seeds contain only minute amounts of sodium, so are ideal for those who need to watch their salt intake. Always buy unsalted nuts and check packets carefully as some seeds are processed with brine (salted water) to clean them. In contrast, the potassium content of nuts is high, which can help to lower high blood pressure.

Low-carbohydrate Most types of nuts and seeds are low-carbohydrate foods, although some contain more than others. Almonds and Brazil nuts have just 1g of carbohydrate per 30g serving, whereas cashew nuts contain around 8g and chestnuts 10g.

High-fibre Nuts are a good source of fibre and contribute to a balanced diet alongside unrefined complex carbohydrate foods, fruit and vegetables. Walnuts, for example, contain 6g fibre per 100g; the same amount as wholemeal (whole-wheat) bread and three times as much as cooked brown rice.

NUTS FOR HEART HEALTH

Research shows that people who regularly eat nuts have a reduced risk of developing cardiovascular disease. Although they are high-fat foods, the fats in seeds and nuts are mostly monounsaturated and polyunsaturated and eating just three or four small handfuls a week as part of a healthy diet can reduce your risk of having a heart attack by up to 50 per cent. While the type of nut isn't that important, some have more heart-healthy nutrients than others.

Unsaturated fats Both polyunsaturated and monounsaturated fats can reduce cholesterol by lowering the 'bad' low-density lipoprotein (LDL) and raising the 'good' high-density lipoprotein levels. High LDL is one of the primary causes of heart disease.

Plant sterols Nuts, especially peanuts, almonds and walnuts and seeds – including sunflower, pumpkin and sesame seeds – contain plant sterols, a substance that can help lower cholesterol. In addition, most nuts (with the exception of pine nuts and coconut) contain linoleic acid, which counteracts cholesterol deposits, and L-arginine, which improves the health of artery walls by making them more flexible and therefore less prone to blood clots, which can block the flow of blood.

Fibre Nuts are a good source of fibre, which helps to lower cholesterol. In addition, it makes you feel full and can suppress your appetite.

Omega-3 fatty acids Many nuts are rich in these fatty acids, which can prevent irregular heart rhythms that can lead to heart attacks.

Vitamin E This vitamin helps to stop the development of plaque in the arteries, which causes them to narrow.

NUTS FOR DIABETES

For diabetics and those with pre-diabetes, it is important to control blood-glucose levels to reduce the long-term risk of high blood pressure, hardening of the arteries and coronary heart disease, stroke, and eye and kidney problems. Research has shown that eating nuts can improve blood-sugar levels in those who are non-insulin dependent or have type 2 diabetes. Choose unsalted nuts without added sugars.

▼ Eating just a small quantity of nuts and seeds every day can have a positive impact on your health.

ALL KINDS OF NUTS

From the warm and humid Amazon rainforests to the cooler deciduous woods of Europe, nuts grow around the world and have been enjoyed for centuries. Whereas fresh nuts were once only available during the autumn and winter, many are now available year round, either loose or in sealed packets. Some are sold still in their shells, while others may be prepared and ready for use. These may be whole, halved, pieces, shredded, flaked (sliced), chopped or ground, raw or ready-toasted.

ALMONDS

These nuts have a light, delicate flavour that means they are superb for making nut milks and butters. Almond trees are native to the eastern Mediterranean but grow in many other areas where the climate is warm enough to protect the tender spring fruit. They belong to the same family of trees as the apricot, plum and peach, which is why they have such a natural affinity with these fruits. Almonds are widely used in Arab cooking and in regions such as Spain, Sicily, Malta and Portugal, which have all been under Arab influence at some time in their past.

There are two types of almond: sweet and bitter. Among the sweet varieties are the almost heart-shaped Valencia almonds that grow in Spain and Portugal, and Californian almonds, which are slightly flatter and more oval in shape. If you want to get the fullest flavour from almonds, buy them unblanched, still in their papery brown skins, as these help retain the moisture and sweetness of the nuts during storage. Bitter almonds are much smaller, bitter to the taste and toxic if eaten raw, so are never sold in stores. The toxins are destroyed by heat and the nuts are used to produce oils and extracts that can be used in baking to add an intense almond flavour.

Health benefits If you need to avoid dairy, calcium-rich almonds should be top of your nut list, to ensure you get plenty of this bone-building mineral. They are the best choice for vitamin E, a natural antioxidant that prevents cell damage and is great for your skin. Vitamin E also reduces the risk of heart disease and possibly health conditions such as age-related cognitive decline. Also good for: protein, iron, magnesium, potassium and zinc.

BRAZIL NUTS

Harvested from huge trees that grow wild in the Amazon rainforest and other parts of South America, Brazil nuts are, botanically, seeds rather than nuts. Between 12 and 20 of these seeds develop inside a hard woody fruit, packed tightly together, hence their wedge shape. The nuts have a sweet milky taste and a high fat content (about 65 per cent), so should always be stored in the refrigerator to prevent them from becoming rancid.

◀ Almonds and cashew nuts are among the most popular types of nut used for making milks.

▲ **Above left** Brazil nuts are rich in selenium, which has many different health-boosting properties. **Above right** Bright-orange cashew apples and their pendulous nuts are important foods in many tropical countries.

Health benefits Brazil nuts are one of the best food sources of the mineral selenium, an antioxidant enzyme that protects against damage from free radicals and the harmful effects of toxic substances such as cigarette smoke and pollution. Selenium increases resistance to infections and also has anti-inflammatory properties. Recent research has shown that it may protect against prostate cancer and thyroid problems. Just one or two Brazil nuts a day will provide sufficient selenium, so add small quantities when making other nut milks and butters for a nutrient boost, or just eat them raw. Don't consume large amounts of Brazil nuts on a daily basis, however, as an excess can lead to hair and nail loss; four should be the maximum amount eaten each day. Also good for: protein, calcium, potassium, zinc, vitamin E and fibre.

CASHEW NUTS

Indigenous to evergreen trees in Brazil, cashew nuts are now widely grown in warm tropical climates. The soft-textured kidney-shaped nuts hang underneath the bright orange fruit known as 'cashew apples' that are similar to a pear in shape. In Brazil, the fruit is made into juice or fermented into an alcoholic drink. The nuts are always sold shelled and very lightly roasted, as this destroys the caustic oil between the two layers of the nut's shell. Cashew nuts make subtle, almost flavourless nut milk. About 10 per cent of the weight is starchy carbohydrate, which helps thicken the milk, making it a versatile cooking ingredient.

Health benefits Especially good for vegans, cashew nuts contain high amounts of both iron, which helps the blood transport oxygen, and zinc, which is great for the immune system. Zinc is not stored by the body, so a daily intake is needed. Also good for: protein, potassium, magnesium, vitamin B6 – needed to metabolize amino acids and fats – and folate, which is important for pregnant women.

CHESTNUTS

Often associated with Christmas, chestnuts are native to southern Europe, parts of Asia and north Africa and are also widely grown in the USA. The shiny brown nuts come from the 'sweet chestnut' and not the 'horse chestnut' tree, which is unrelated and whose nuts are inedible. Most are imported from France and Spain. Excellent in both savoury and sweet dishes, the fresh nuts are often sold in their shells in the autumn and winter, but whole, cooked, peeled chestnuts as well as puréed ones can be bought vacuum-packed or in cans and jars all year round, although they are most readily available in December as they are a part of European Christmas traditions. Chestnuts have a low fat content and a soft floury texture and should always be eaten cooked. As a rough guide, 675g/1½lb unpeeled chestnuts will yield 450g/1lb peeled chestnuts. They can be fiddly to prepare, so for speed use pre-prepared ones.

Health benefits By far the nut with the lowest fat and calorie content, chestnuts contain a greater amount of starchy carbohydrates than most other nuts and are also a good source of vitamin C (take care not to overcook them or this can be destroyed). Also good for: B-vitamins, including B6.

▼ **Below left** Chestnuts can be bought fresh or pre-prepared. **Below centre** Coconuts yield a wide range of useful cooking products. **Below right** Hazelnuts are lower in fat than many other types of nut.

COCONUTS

A popular ingredient in Asian, South American and African cuisines, coconut adds a sweet, creamy flavour to dishes. One of the world's most versatile foods, the content of a coconut's fibrous husk is the source of an enormous range of versatile ingredients. Coconuts come from the coconut palm tree, which grows well only in warm, sunny, humid climates. The white flesh can be made into coconut milk and cream, blended to make coconut butter or shredded and dried to make flakes and desiccated (dry unsweetened shredded) coconut.

Health benefits Although the fat in coconut is mainly saturated, recent research has shown that coconuts are rich in medium-chain fatty acids, which are digested in a similar manner to carbohydrates rather than fat. Coconut can also increase HDL levels (the 'good' cholesterol). Also good for: vitamins C and E, both of which fight free radical damage in the body.

HAZELNUTS

Grown in Britain, the USA, Turkey, Spain and Italy, hazelnuts are usually sold as shelled whole nuts, sometimes with their papery brown skins still on. They have a distinctive flavour that is intensified by roasting, which also makes it easy to rub off the skins. Filberts and cobnuts (traditionally grown in Kent, England) are both types of cultivated hazelnuts. Cobnuts are sold in their freshly-picked state, with a pale green and tan shell and often still in the green leafy husk. The kernels are milky and moist.

▲ Crisp and creamy, macadamia nuts are a luxurious treat and usually come with a price tag that reflects this.

▲ Peanuts are available in many forms: in their shells, shelled and in or out of their skins, and as butter or milk.

Hazelnut oil is a rich-tasting deep brown oil that can be used together with hazelnuts to make flavoursome nut butter.

Health benefits One of the healthiest nuts, hazelnuts are lower in fat than most other types. They are a good source of oleic acid, which can help reduce blood pressure. Also good for: vitamin E, folate and fibre.

MACADAMIA NUTS

Native to Australia, macadamia nuts are a major cultivated crop in Hawaii, where over 90 per cent of the world's macadamias are now produced. Small quantities are also grown in California and South America. Buttery and rich, these crisp-textured round nuts contain more fat than any other type and are fairly expensive.

Health benefits Macadamia nuts are high in oil, but this is 78 per cent unsaturated and mainly monounsaturated, and they contain a particularly high amount of omega-3 fatty acids, which protect the heart. They have more than double the amount of fibre of most nuts. Also good for: Thiamin (B1), which is needed for the release of energy, omega 3, calcium and potassium.

PEANUTS

Despite their name, peanut aren't nuts at all, but a legume that grows in warm climates. They are native to South America, but vast amounts are now produced in China and, to a lesser extent, in India and the USA. Peanuts develop just below the surface of the soil after the plant has flowered, which is why they are also known as groundnuts. A large proportion of the crop is made into groundnut oil (the nuts contain nearly 50 per cent oil) and huge quantities are also used commercially to make peanut butter. In some countries, notably parts of Africa, peanuts are a staple food and are made into stews. The light porous shell of the peanut allows the nut to easily absorb substances from the soil, including pesticides, so ideally you should buy organic ones.

Health benefits Peanuts contain more protein per gram than any other nut. They also have good amounts of niacin (vitamin B3), which can help lower blood-cholesterol levels, and folate – essential for brain development and which may protect against cognitive decline and birth defects in unborn babies. Also good for: fibre, iron, potassium and vitamin E.

▲ **Above left** Pine nuts are widely used in Middle Eastern and Mediterranean cooking. **Top right** Pecan nuts lower cholesterol and help release energy from food. **Above right** Pistachios are a good source of vitamin B6.

PECAN NUTS

The species that produces pecan nuts is the only major nut tree to grow naturally in North America, predominantly in the Deep South, and the name originates from the native-American word 'paccan', used to describe any nut that needed to be cracked open with a stone. Traditionally used in many American recipes, notably pecan pie, the nuts have glossy reddish-brown oval shells with double-lobed kernels similar to elongated walnuts, but are smoother, softer and slightly sweeter in taste. **Health benefits** These are especially heart-healthy and contain high amounts of sterols, which can lower cholesterol levels. They are also an excellent source of vitamin B3, which helps to fight fatigue as it assists in breaking down energy from food. Also good for: vitamin E, zinc and oleic acid.

PINE NUTS

These are the edible nuts of the pine tree: either the Korean pine, which produces small tear-shaped nuts; or the Mediterranean stone pine, which produces longer, more slender nuts. Difficult to harvest, a ton of pine cones yields less than 39kg/85lb of these tiny nuts, so inevitably they are very expensive to buy. With their creamy, almost golden, colour, the nuts have a buttery-soft texture and delicate aromatic taste that is even more delicious toasted. Popular in Middle Eastern cooking, they are also a key ingredient of Italian pesto, for which they are blended together with garlic, rich olive oil and fragrant fresh basil to make a distinctive, aromatic sauce. If you are buying pine nuts loose, make sure they are really fresh as they have a very high fat content (almost 70 per cent) and turn rancid quickly. **Health benefits** Pine nuts are an excellent source of thiamin (vitamin B1) as well as phosphorus. Also good for: protein and iron, and they contain moderate amounts of niacin (vitamin B3).

▲ Mature walnuts have many culinary uses or can be simply cracked open and enjoyed raw.

PISTACHIO NUTS

These small nuts are pale green – sometimes with patches of vibrant green – and have a thin purplish-red skin, most of which is removed when the nuts are shelled. Prized as much for their colour as their flavour, they may also be bought in split shells, but these are usually salted, so unsuitable for making into nut milk; make sure you buy unsalted ones.
Health benefits Pistachios contain vitamin B6, iron and potassium – useful in helping to lower blood pressure. Also good for: protein, calcium, iron, thiamin (B1) and vitamin E.

WALNUTS

Although grown in many parts of the world, most walnuts are imported from France, Italy and California. When they are picked young in the summer months, the walnut is referred to as 'wet'; the walnuts are green and fleshy with fresh milky kernels and the shells are soft and jelly-like and not yet set: they can be preserved in this way as a pickle. In the autumn months the shell hardens inside the green fruit.

The nuts have a bitter-sweet flavour and can be bought shelled as walnut halves or pieces; the latter tend to be slightly cheaper and are excellent for making nut milks and butters.
Health benefits All nuts contain omega-3 fats, but walnuts have particularly high amounts of alpha linoleic acid (ALA) as well. This can help irregular heart patterns, which are a major cause of heart attacks. Walnuts reduce inflammation and oxidation in the arteries. Also good for: magnesium and phosphorus, which is needed alongside calcium to build strong bones and teeth.

NUTS OR SEEDS?

A nut is a dried tree fruit contained in a hard shell, whereas a seed is the embryo and food supply of a new plant. Many foods that we refer to as 'nuts' aren't really nuts at all. Pine trees produce cones that contain seeds that aren't enclosed in a shell, so pine 'nuts' are actually seeds. Peanuts are also really seeds, or 'legumes', since they develop inside a legume or pod. This is pushed below the ground by the plant and eventually becomes dry and hard and much like a nut in terms of culinary usage. A coconut isn't a true nut either, but is a large fruit known as a 'drupe'.

ALL KINDS OF SEEDS

Seeds may look small and unexciting but, like nuts, they are packed with goodness and make superbly rich and creamy seed milks and butters.

SESAME SEEDS

These tiny white or black seeds are popular in Middle Eastern and Oriental cooking. They can be ground to a thick paste to make tahini or Chinese sesame-seed paste, depending on whether the seeds are toasted first. They are also ground to make halvah, a tooth-achingly sweet confection enjoyed in many countries, including Greece, Turkey and Israel.

Health benefits Sesame seeds are rich in protein and calcium. Also good for: iron and niacin (vitamin B3).

SUNFLOWER SEEDS

As the name suggests, sunflower seeds are the seeds of the sunflower. These huge yellow flowers, originally from Mexico and Peru, are an important crop in many parts of the world, especially Russia and the Ukraine. They are grown for their seeds and the oil that can be made from them, although they are sometimes cultivated as a cut flower. The whole of the plant can be used: the cake of crushed seeds left behind after the oil is removed is fed to farm animals; extracts from the leaves can be used to treat diseases such as malaria; and the stems are used as a compost.

Health benefits These seeds are rich in potassium and phosphorus and contain poly-phenol compounds, such as chlorogenic acid, quinic acid and caffeic acids, all of which are natural anti-oxidants. Chlorogenic acid helps reduce blood-sugar levels, so this is particularly useful for diabetics. Also good for: iron, zinc and vitamins C and E.

▼ **Below left** Sunflower, sesame and pumpkin seeds can all be used to make seed milks. **Below right** Hemp seeds contain all nine essential amino acids.

▲ Pumpkin seeds can be enjoyed raw, toasted or ground to make a thickening agent, as well for milk and butter.

PUMPKIN SEEDS

Olive-green in colour and with a pointed oval shape, pumpkin seeds are the centres of the large white seeds found in the fibrous hearts of pumpkins. They are widely used in South American cooking, for which they are roasted and ground and used to thicken sauces.

Health benefits The zinc content of pumpkin seeds is high, so these are particularly beneficial for supporting the immune system. Also good for: protein, iron and vitamin C.

HEMP SEEDS

Small and brownish-green in colour, hemp seeds have a distinctive flavour. Often confused with marijuana, they come from the same species but are an entirely different plant. Bought whole or hulled, hemp seeds have a long history of cultivation, but fell out of favour. Recent knowledge about their nutritional value has increased their popularity and they are now readily available.

Health benefits These high-protein seeds contain all nine of the essential amino acids, so are especially useful to vegans. They also have a balanced ratio of omega-3 to omega-6 fats (one to three). Also good for: vitamin E.

BUYING AND STORING NUTS AND SEEDS

Shelled nuts and whole seeds are sometimes sold loose in wholefood stores and delicatessens; always buy from a reliable source with a high turnover and check that the nuts are very fresh and not old stock. It is better to buy them in small quantities as and when you need them. Alternatively, they can be bought in plastic sachets from supermarkets and should be used within the use-by date. The high oil content makes nuts prone to rancidity, so they should be stored in a cool, dark place, preferably the refrigerator, or in the freezer if you have the space. In the refrigerator they will keep for at least 3 months, and frozen for at least 6 months. Once packets are opened, decant the nuts into an airtight container (not metal).

Unlike most nuts, chestnuts bought in their shells have been recently picked and are in their fresh, not dried, state. They have a short shelf-life and should be eaten within 10 days of purchase. Seeds should look smooth and not shrivelled and dry. When buying sesame seeds look for ones that have been processed naturally by mechanical rolling. They should have a matt appearance; shiny ones may have been processed chemically.

TOOLS AND EQUIPMENT

Making nut and seed milks and butters requires little specialist equipment and, providing you have a blender or food processor, they can be made simply and quickly. You will probably already own a few other pieces of equipment that will make the process easier, including a calibrated jug (cup), rubber spatula and a sieve (strainer). The following is an outline of the more useful items, all of which are readily available from department and specialist kitchen stores.

BLENDER

Both nut and seed milks and butters can be made in an ordinary blender or food processor, but the results may be slightly grainy. If you want to make ultra-smooth butters, choose a machine with at least 600 watts of power and that has a blade that is suitable for crushing ice (and therefore capable of finely grinding nuts and seeds). While high-powered blenders such as Vitamix are more expensive, they are very powerful and will extract the maximum amount of 'milk' and produce creamy nut butters. Bear in mind that when using such machines for butters, you will need to make large enough quantities for the nuts or seeds to cover the blades of the machine and keep the mixture

▼ **Below left** Nut bags have a fine mesh and produce smooth nut milks. **Below centre** A high-powered blender, such as a Vitamix, is useful for making nut milks. **Bottom right** A baking tray is used for toasting nuts.

moving, at least 400g/14oz/3½ cups of nuts or 300g/10oz/2 cups seeds. If you want to make less than this, a small high-powered food processor will do a better job. You should also check how easy it will be to scoop nut butter from the machine after making; one with a removable blade makes this task (and washing up) much simpler.

NUT BAGS

While nut and seed milks don't have to be strained, a nut bag is a worthwhile investment if you prefer milks with a smooth, silky texture. These re-usable bags have a very fine nylon mesh and are usually in a funnel shape for easy straining. Most have a drawstring so that you can hang the bag to drain. Nut bags are very strong but not unbreakable so, when using, squeeze gently but do not twist the bag. The stitching on most nut bags is on the outside, which makes them easier to clean. After use, rinse the bag well and if necessary wash it in warm soapy water. Rinse thoroughly to remove all traces of detergent and air dry.

JELLY BAG OR MUSLIN (CHEESECLOTH) AND SIEVE

These are alternatives to using a nut bag. Jelly bags are made from calico or nylon and are usually used for straining juices from cooked fruit pulp for preserve-making. The weave is close, although not as fine as that of a nut bag. Some jelly bags come with a stand, which

makes straining easier. Muslin can be used instead of a nut or jelly bag: layer two or three squares in a sieve placed over a bowl, wide jug or pitcher to catch the milk. The sieve should be nylon, plastic or stainless steel, as some metals will taint the milk's flavour.

GLASS JUG OR PITCHER

A glass jug or pitcher is preferable for storing milks, as the flavour can be affected by storing it in a plastic one. Choose one with a closable lid, so that the milk does not get contaminated by other food flavours during storage in the refrigerator; a jug or pitcher with a screw-lid and with a pouring spout is preferable.

JARS AND CONTAINERS

When storing nut butters, clear glass jars are ideal as you can see the contents easily. Be sure to choose ones that are appropriately shaped and sized; wide-necked ones make filling and using much easier. Most nut butters will keep for several weeks in the refrigerator, but can also be frozen in freezerproof containers.

CALIBRATED JUG AND MEASURING SPOONS

For measuring the amount of water needed when making milks, a calibrated measuring jug is essential. You should also use accurate measuring spoons for other ingredients, such as oil and various sweeteners. If you make a note of the quantities used for nut and seed milks and butters, you can tweak quantities to suit your personal preferences when you next make the milk or butter.

SPATULAS

A flexible rubber or plastic spatula can be used to scrape the last bits of nut or seed butter from the food processor or blender after you have made it. It also avoids damaging or scratching the jug, pitcher or bowl of the machine.

STERILIZING JARS

It is a good idea to sterilize jars before using them, to destroy any micro-organisms that might affect the nut or seed butter, particularly if you are re-using a jar. The simplest way is to put the jars and lids in a dishwasher and run it on the hottest setting, including drying. Alternatively, you can sterilize them in the oven or microwave:

Oven method Stand the jars, spaced slightly apart, on a baking sheet lined with kitchen paper. Rest any lids on top. Place in a cold oven, then heat to 110°C/225°F/ Gas ¼ and heat for 30 minutes. Leave to cool completely before filling.

Microwave method Half-fill the clean jars with water and heat on Full Power, until the water has boiled for at least 1 minute. Using oven gloves (mitts), remove the jars from the microwave. Carefully swirl the water inside them, then pour it away. Drain the jars upside-down on a clean dish towel, then turn upright and leave to dry.

BAKING SHEET AND NON-STICK FRYING PAN

A baking sheet is useful when oven-roasting nuts or seeds prior to making butters. Choose one with sides, so the nuts or seeds won't roll off, and use a good-quality heavy one that won't buckle at high temperatures or develop hot-spots that might cause burning. Avoid baking sheets that are very dark as they absorb more heat, which means nuts and seeds burn more easily. You can also toast them in a non-stick frying pan on the hob.

MAKING NUT MILKS

While store-bought cartons of nut milk are convenient, they may contain a higher proportion of sugar than nuts, as well as additional ingredients such as thickeners, preservatives and flavourings. Home-made nut milks are healthy, fresh, unprocessed and additive-free. Often more economical than commercially-made nut milks, they allow you to have complete control of the quality of ingredients included and the final taste, texture and thickness of the milk.

A range of nut-based 'milks' can be made simply by blending shelled raw unsalted nuts with water. Cashew nuts, almonds, peanuts, chestnuts, coconuts, Brazil nuts, hazelnuts, macadamia nuts, pecans and pistachios can all be liquefied into deliciously creamy milks. These can be used neat as a drink or in cooking, or made into a selection of other dairy-free ingredients, such as cream, yogurt or 'cheese'. They can also be flavoured or sweetened with natural foods such as dates, agave or cacao.

CASHEW NUT MILK

Milk made from cashews has an almost neutral flavour, which means it is ideal if you want to blend it with other flavourings (see pages 34–7), or use it in cooking without adding a distinctly nutty flavour. Because cashews are a relatively 'soft' nut, they require only a short soaking time, but if it is more convenient, you can leave them to soak overnight.

Simple cashew nut milk

This six-step method of making a basic nut milk can be applied to most types of nuts, although the soaking time for each will vary (see page 22).

175g/6oz/1¼ cups raw unsalted cashew nuts
750ml/1¼ pints/3 cups filtered water, plus soaking water
pinch of sea salt (optional)

Makes about 800ml/1 pint 7fl oz/3¼ cups

1 Put the cashew nuts in a large glass, ceramic or stainless steel bowl. Pour over enough water to cover by about 2.5cm/1in. Filtered water is preferable, as filtering removes impurities that may spoil the flavour of the milk, but you can use bottled or tap water. Add a small pinch of sea salt as well if you like; this will help soften the nuts, but isn't essential and should be left out if you are on a low-sodium diet. Leave to soak at room temperature for 3–6 hours.

2 After soaking, strain the cashew nuts, then rinse them and tip them into a blender with a capacity of at least 1.5 litres/2½ pints/6¼ cups.

3 Add about a third of the water (250ml/8fl oz/ 1 cup) to the blender. Pulse a few times to break up the nuts, then blend continuously for about 1 minute. Add a further 250ml/7fl oz/1 cup water and blend for a further minute, until the

▲ Nut milk can be made from a wide range of different nuts, from mild-flavoured cashew nuts and almonds to bright-green pistachio nuts, Brazil nuts and decadently rich macadamia nuts.

mixture is well-blended and smooth. A high-powered blender such as a Vitamix is preferable to finely pulverize the nuts. If you are using a less powerful machine, you will need to blend the mixture for 1–2 minutes more.

4 Strain the liquid to give it a silkier texture and remove any fine pieces of nuts that haven't completely blended. Pour the mixture through a very fine-meshed plastic or stainless steel sieve (strainer) into a large bowl. For a smoother end result, line the sieve with a layer of muslin (cheesecloth), or pour the liquid through a re-usable nut bag placed over a bowl, jug or pitcher. Leave it to filter for a few minutes, then gently stir the pulp to encourage the liquid to pass through more quickly. To extract a little more nut milk, slowly pour the remaining water over the pulp and leave it to drain again.

5 Squeeze the last of the milk from the nut pulp. When the milk has filtered through, gather up the corners of the muslin or nut bag and squeeze it with clean hands to extract the last few drops of milk. The damp nut pulp can be made into nut 'flour' (see pages 38–9).

6 If you want to serve the nut milk at once as a drink, pour it over a few ice cubes in a glass. Otherwise pour the milk into a glass jug or pitcher, cover and store it in the refrigerator.

▲ Soaking nuts before blending them not only results in a higher yield, but also releases beneficial enzymes.

▲ Different nuts require different soaking times, depending on how hard or soft they are.

WHY NUTS SHOULD BE SOAKED

It is possible to make nut milk by blending unsoaked raw nuts with water, but for most types it is preferable to soak them first, even if only for a short time. Some, including cashew and macadamia nuts, are softer, so need less soaking than harder ones, such as almonds. All nuts will absorb some water during soaking, which softens them so that they will yield more 'milk' than if they were processed without being soaked. Soaking also stimulates the germination process, causing beneficial enzymes to be activated and released into the milk. In moderate conditions, nuts should be soaked at room temperature, but if the weather is hot, or you are soaking them for more than 12 hours, cover the bowl of nuts and water with clear film (plastic wrap) and put it in the refrigerator.

NUT SOAKING TIMES

Almonds	8–24 hours
Cashew and macadamia nuts	3–6 hours
Brazil and pistachio nuts	1–4 hours
Hazelnuts and peanuts	6–8 hours
Walnuts and pecan nuts	4–6 hours

NUT MILK STORAGE AND SHELF LIFE

Home-made nut milk should be kept in the refrigerator in a glass jug or pitcher with a lid or covered with clear film. Avoid plastic or metal as these can taint the flavour. It will stay fresh for up to 3 days. After a day or two, the milk may separate, so give it a stir before using. If you are unable to use up all the milk in this time, it can be frozen and it is also possible to pasteurize nut milk, so that it will keep for up to a week. Heat the milk to just below boiling point, then maintain the temperature for 3–4 minutes. Cool the milk quickly by putting the pan in a bowl of iced water. Pasteurization will affect the flavour of the milk and destroy some vitamins, so it is better to only make what you will drink within a few days.

MAKING MILKS OF DIFFERENT STRENGTHS

Making your own nut milk allows you to decide on the final texture and thickness of the milk. For most uses, a medium-bodied milk works well, but you can also make richer, creamier ones or opt for more economical light-bodied milks, simply by adapting the ratio of nuts to water. You can also leave nut milks unstrained if you prefer a more textured liquid.

Full-bodied blends These are ideal for making rich custards and ice creams or for maximum flavour. Full-bodied blends can be used to replace single (light) cream in many recipes. Use 225g/8oz/1⅓ cups nuts for every 750ml/1¼ pints/3 cups water.

Medium-bodied blends These are ideal for drinking on their own, for serving with breakfast cereals, and to replace dairy milk in cooking. Use 175g/6oz/1 cup nuts for every 750ml/1¼ pints/3 cups water.

Light-bodied blends The most economical to make, these can be used on cereals and as a base in milkshakes and smoothies. Use 75g/3oz/½ cup nuts for every 750ml/1¼ pints/3 cups water.

THICKENING AND EMULSIFYING NUT MILKS

It is normal for nut milks to separate slightly after you have stored them in the refrigerator for a day or two; you simply need to stir them before using. Alternatively, you can add a natural emulsifier, such as lecithin, to the milk.

Lecithin This creamy-beige coloured powder (also available as granules) is a derivative of the soy bean and acts as a thickener and emulsifier, helping to prevent the milk from separating. It will also lengthen the keeping time of the milk by a day or two. Lecithin is needed by every living cell in the human body and is a natural source of inositol and choline; two nutrients that play an important role in fat metabolism. It helps the body break down and dispose of low-density lipoprotein (LDL) cholesterol. Some claim it can help promote weight loss, although this benefit is still controversial.

Tocotrienols Also known as 'rice solubles', these are also a natural and beneficial additive and are excellent for thickening the milk. Rich in vitamin E, they add a subtle sweetness. Up to 30ml/2 tbsp of lecithin and/or tocotrienols can be blended into every 800ml/1 pint 7fl oz/3¼ cups nut milk after it has been strained.

▼ Nut milks may require a quick stir before use if they have been stored in the refrigerator for a few days.

ALMOND MILK

The most popular and widely consumed nut milk, almond milk has a silky-smooth texture and creamy taste as well as fantastic nutritional benefits. Its mild flavour makes it superb for drinking, pouring over cereals and for cooking, and because almonds have an affinity with many fruits, such as apricots, peaches and raspberries, it is especially good when making fruity desserts. It also works well with chocolate and coffee.

Simple unsweetened almond milk

Buy shelled almonds in their skins for the best flavour, then blanch them yourself (see box) before making this milk. This recipe makes a medium-thickness simple almond milk.

175g/6oz/1 cup raw unsalted blanched almonds
750ml/1¼ pints/3 cups filtered water, plus soaking water

Makes about 800ml/1 pint 7fl oz/3¼ cups

1 Put the almonds in a large glass, ceramic or stainless steel bowl. Pour over enough water to cover by about 2.5cm/1in. Leave to soak at room temperature for at least 8 hours or place in the refrigerator and soak for up to 24 hours.

2 Drain and rinse the almonds, then tip them into a blender and add 250ml/8fl oz/1 cup water. Pulse a few times to break up the nuts, then blend continuously for 1 minute. Add a further 250ml/8fl oz/1 cup water and blend for 1–3 minutes or until the mixture is smooth.

3 Pour the mixture through a nut bag hung over a jug, pitcher or bowl and leave to drain for a few minutes. Slowly pour in the rest of the water and leave to drain again. Gently squeeze the nut bag to extract all the milk. If you don't have a nut bag, pour the mixture through a sieve (strainer) lined with muslin (cheesecloth).

4 When the milk has filtered through, gather up the corners of the muslin or nut bag and gently squeeze with clean hands to extract the last few drops of nut the milk. The slightly damp nut pulp can be made into nut 'flour' (see pages 38–9). Store the milk, covered, in a jug or pitcher in the refrigerator for up to 4 days.

HOW TO BLANCH ALMONDS

Removing the brown papery skins from almonds is known as 'blanching'. This technique should be done just before you start soaking the almonds to make almond milk, as blanching will start the softening process that is continued when you leave the nuts to soak.

1 Put the almonds in a heatproof bowl and pour over enough boiling water to cover the nuts by about 2.5cm/1in. Leave to soak until the water is tepid and the almonds cool enough to handle.

2 Drain the almonds, then squeeze the nuts out of the brown skins; they should slide out easily. Discard the skins.

Light almond milk

In this recipe, fewer almonds are used than for simple unsweetened almond milk, and lecithin is added to give the milk a slightly thicker texture and to reduce separation. You may wish to add a few drops of vanilla extract to the milk and a little sweetener, as light nut milk blends can benefit from additional flavouring. This is an excellent economical nut milk for using as a base for milkshakes and smoothies and for making or serving with cereals such as porridge and granola.

75g/3oz/½ cup raw unsalted blanched almonds
750ml/1¼ pints/3 cups filtered water, plus soaking water
30ml/2 tbsp powdered lecithin
2.5ml/½ tsp vanilla extract (optional)
5ml/1 tsp agave syrup or clear honey

Makes about 800ml/1 pint 7fl oz/3¼ cups

1 Put the blanched almonds in a large glass, ceramic or stainless steel bowl. Pour over enough water to cover by about 2.5cm/1in. Leave to soak at room temperature for at least 8 hours or place in the refrigerator and soak for up to 24 hours.

2 Drain the almonds and rinse, then tip them into a blender and add 250ml/8fl oz/1 cup water. Pulse a few times to break up the nuts, then blend continuously for 1 minute. Add a further 250ml/8fl oz/1 cup water and blend for 1–3 minutes or until the mixture is smooth.

▲ You can adapt the thickness and flavour of almond milk to suit your preferences and requirements.

3 Pour the mixture through a nut bag suspended over a jug, pitcher or bowl and leave to drain for a few minutes. Slowly pour in the rest of the water and leave to drain again. Finally, gently squeeze the nut bag to extract all the milk. If you don't have a nut bag pour the mixture through a muslin-lined sieve or colander. When the milk has filtered through, gather up the corners of the muslin or nut bag and gently squeeze with clean hands to extract the last few drops of nut milk. The slightly damp nut pulp can be made into nut 'flour' (see pages 38–9).

4 Pour the almond milk back into a clean blender. Add the lecithin, vanilla extract and agave syrup or honey, if using, then blend again. Store the milk, covered, in a jug or pitcher in the refrigerator for up to 4 days.

OTHER NUT MILKS

In addition to almond and cashew nut milks, you can easily make a range of other delectable milks from different types of nuts. These bring their own unique flavours, nutrients, textures and colours to the table.

Hazelnut milk

This is one of the few nut milks that benefits from being made with lightly roasted rather than raw nuts. You can buy ready-toasted whole or chopped hazelnuts, but you get a much better flavour if you roast your own. If you buy hazelnuts in their skins, follow the instructions in the box below to roast and skin them, then follow the recipe from step 2. If you buy skinned hazelnuts, you can roast them for a little less time to make a lighter-coloured and more subtly-flavoured milk. Some of the flavour will leach into the soaking water, so here the nuts aren't drained after being soaked.

175g/6oz/1 cup raw unsalted skinned hazelnuts
750ml/1¼ pints/3 cups filtered water

Makes about 800ml/1 pint 7fl oz/3¼ cups

1 Spread the hazelnuts in a single layer on a baking sheet. Bake at 180°C/350°F/Gas 4 for 7–8 minutes; they should be very lightly browned and smell nutty. Watch them carefully as over-roasting will make the nuts bitter. Leave the nuts to cool, then tip them into a bowl and pour over the water. Soak for 6–8 hours.

2 Tip the nuts and about half of their soaking water into a blender. Pulse a few times to break up the nuts, then blend continuously for 1 minute. Add the remaining water and blend for 2–3 minutes or until the mixture is smooth.

3 Pour through a nut bag suspended over a jug, pitcher or bowl and leave to drain. If you don't have a nut bag, pour the mixture through a sieve (strainer) lined with muslin (cheesecloth).

4 When the milk has filtered through, gather up the nut bag or the corners of the muslin and gently squeeze with clean hands to extract the last few drops of nut milk. The slightly damp nut pulp can be made into nut 'flour' (see pages 38–9). Store the milk, covered, in a jug or pitcher in the refrigerator for up to 4 days.

ROASTING AND SKINNING HAZELNUTS

Oven-roasting hazelnuts and other nuts develops their delicious and unique nutty flavour. It also enables the thin reddish-brown outer skin to be easily removed.

1 Place the nuts in a single layer on a baking sheet. Bake at 180°C/350°F/Gas 4 for 10–12 minutes or until the skins begin to split and the nuts are golden.

2 Leave the nuts to cool for a few minutes, then tip them on to a clean dish towel and rub vigorously to loosen and remove the skins.

Walnut or pecan nut milk

Walnuts are less sweet than many other nuts and sometimes have a hint of bitterness. Soaking will eliminate this. Pecans are similar but have a slightly sweeter taste.

115g/4oz/1¼ cup raw unsalted walnuts or pecans
700ml/1 pint 3fl oz/2¾ cups filtered water,
  plus soaking water

Makes about 750ml/1¼ pints/3 cups

1 Put the nuts in a large glass, ceramic or stainless steel bowl. Pour over enough water to cover by 2.5cm/1in. Leave to soak at room temperature for 4–6 hours. Drain and rinse.

2 Pulse the nuts and one-third of the water a few times, then blend continuously for 1 minute. Add one-third more of water. Blend for 2–3 minutes, until smooth.

3 Pour the mixture through a nut bag or a muslin-lined sieve suspended over a bowl and leave to drain. Pour in the rest of the water and leave to drain again.

4 Gently squeeze the nut bag or muslin with clean hands to extract the last drops. Discard the pulp. Store in the refrigerator, covered, for up to 3 days.

Macadamia nut milk

High in fat, macadamias are soft enough to make a rich nut milk without the need for soaking, although the yield will be slightly higher if you soak the nuts first.

115g/4oz/¾ cup raw unsalted macadamia nuts
350ml/12fl oz/1½ cups filtered water,
  plus soaking water

Makes about 400ml/14fl oz/1⅔ cups

1 Put the nuts in a large glass, ceramic or stainless steel bowl. Pour over enough water to cover by 2.5cm/1in. Leave to soak at room temperature for 3–6 hours.

2 Drain and rinse the nuts. Pulse them with 250ml/8fl oz/1 cup water a few times, then blend continuously for 1 minute. Blend for 2–3 minutes, until smooth.

3 Pour the mixture through a nut bag or a muslin-lined sieve suspended over a jug or pitcher and leave to drain. Pour in the remaining water and leave to drain again.

4 Squeeze the nut bag or muslin with clean hands to extract the last drops. Discard the pulp. Cover and store in the refrigerator for up to 3 days.

Pistachio milk

Since pistachios are expensive, this milk is best served in small quantities and used where it will play a starring role. Soaking is not essential but it will maximize the yield.

115g/4oz/¾ cup raw unsalted pistachio nuts
350ml/12fl oz/1½ cups filtered water,
    plus soaking water

Makes about 400ml/14fl oz/1⅔ cups

1 Put the nuts in a glass, ceramic or stainless steel bowl. Pour over enough water to cover by about 2.5cm/1in. Leave to soak at room temperature for 1–4 hours. Drain and rinse.

2 Use a small sharp knife to remove any remaining skin. Blend the nuts with 250ml/8fl oz/1 cup water. Pulse a few times, then blend continuously for 1–2 minutes, until smooth.

3 Pour the mixture through a nut bag or a sieve (strainer) lined with muslin (cheesecloth) over a bowl, jug or pitcher and leave to drain. Pour in the rest of the water. Leave to drain.

4 Gently squeeze the nut bag or muslin with clean hands.The nut pulp makes excellent nut 'flour' (see pages 38–9). Chill, covered, for up to 3 days.

Brazil nut milk

Selenium-rich Brazil nuts make a creamy, mild-flavoured, almost white milk. It is particularly good blended with tropical fruit such as bananas or goji berries.

75g/3oz/½ cup raw unsalted Brazil nuts
550ml/18fl oz/2½ cups filtered water,
    plus soaking water

Makes about 600ml/1 pint/2½ cups

1 Put the nuts in a large glass, ceramic or stainless steel bowl. Pour over enough water to cover by 2.5cm/1in. Leave to soak at room temperature for 1–4 hours. Drain and rinse.

2 Put the nuts in a blender with 250ml/8fl oz/1 cup water. Pulse a few times, then add another 250ml/8fl oz/1 cup water. Blend for 1–2 minutes, until the mixture is smooth.

3 Pour the mixture through a nut bag or a strainer lined with muslin over a bowl, jug or pitcher and leave to drain. Pour in the rest of the water. Leave to drain.

4 Gently squeeze the nut bag or muslin with clean hands. Reserve the nut pulp to make nut 'flour' (see pages 38–9). Chill, covered, for up to 3 days.

Chestnut milk

Unlike other nuts, chestnuts are high in carbohydrates and low in fat. They make a thick pale-brown milk with very little leftover nut pulp. The quickest and easiest method is to use ready-cooked and peeled vacuum-packed chestnuts, but you can use and prepare fresh ones if you prefer (see the box below).

175g/6oz/1 cup cooked and peeled chestnuts
750ml/1¼ pints/3 cups filtered water

Makes about 800ml/1 pint 7fl oz/3¼ cups

1 Halve the cooked, peeled chestnuts (or prepare 250g/9oz/1⅓ cups fresh ones, following the instructions in the box to the right).

2 Pulse the nuts in a blender with the water a few times to break them up, then blend continuously for 2–3 minutes or until the mixture is smooth.

3 Pour the mixture through a nut bag suspended over a jug, pitcher or bowl and leave to drain. If you don't have a nut bag, pour the mixture through a muslin-lined sieve.

4 When the milk has filtered through, gather up the nut bag or muslin and gently squeeze with clean hands to extract the last few drops of nut milk. Discard the nut pulp. Store the chestnut milk, covered, in the refrigerator and use within 3 days of making.

▲ Low-fat chestnut milk has a distinctive appearance and flavour, and a thick consistency.

PEELING CHESTNUTS

Fresh chestnuts are often roasted in the oven but it is preferable to boil them for chestnut milk, to keep them moist.

1 Slit the rounded shell of each nut with a sharp knife and place the chestnuts in a large pan. Cover with cold water, bring to a boil and cook for 15 minutes. Turn off the heat and leave to stand for 5 minutes.

2 Remove a few nuts at a time with a slotted spoon. When they are cool enough to handle, peel them with a sharp knife, removing the outer shell and all the slightly furry brown skin. Leave the remaining chestnuts in the hot water until you are ready to peel them so that they stay warm and soft.

MAKING SEED AND GRAIN MILKS

Delicious healthy milks can be made from seeds, such as pumpkin and sunflower seeds, and grains including oats and hemp. While most seeds benefit from long soaking, others like hemp seeds need little or no soaking, so milks made from these can be ready to use in a very short amount of time.

Sunflower or pumpkin seed milk

Packed with protein, vitamins and minerals, sunflower and pumpkin seeds are high in fat, so make rich, creamy milks. Seed milks tend to oxidize more quickly than nut milks, so for maximum nutritional benefit consume them within 2 days of making them.

75g/3oz/½ cup sunflower or pumpkin seeds
350ml/12fl oz/1½ cups filtered water, plus soaking water

Makes about 400ml/14fl oz/1⅔ cups

1 Put the seeds in a bowl and pour in enough water to cover by about 2.5cm/1in. Leave to soak at room temperature for at least 8 hours, or place in the refrigerator and soak for up to 14 hours.

2 Drain and rinse the seeds, then tip them into a blender and add 300ml/½ pint/1¼ cups of the filtered water. Pulse the blender a few times to break up the seeds, then blend continuously for 2–3 minutes or until smooth.

▲ Seeds are generally cheaper than nuts, and can be used to make equally nutritious and delicious milks.

3 Pour the mixture through a nut bag over a jug, pitcher or bowl and leave to drain for a few minutes. When the milk has drained through, add the rest of the water and drain again. If you don't have a nut bag, use a sieve (strainer) lined with muslin (cheesecloth).

4 When the milk has filtered through, gather up the corners of the nut bag or muslin and gently squeeze with clean hands to extract the last few drops of seed milk. The slightly damp seed pulp can be made into seed 'flour' (see pages 38–9). Store, covered, in the refrigerator and use within 2 days; ideally sunflower seed milk should be used within 24 hours of making; pumpkin seed milk will keep well for 2 days.

Hemp seed milk

An excellent source of protein, hemp seeds provide all nine essential amino acids, so this milk is particularly beneficial for vegans. Don't add more seeds than suggested or the milk may have a bitter aftertaste.

50g/2oz/⅓ cup hemp seeds
475ml/16fl oz/2 cups filtered water

Makes about 500ml/17fl oz/generous 2 cups

1 Put the seeds and water in a blender. Pulse a few times to start breaking up the seeds, then blend continuously for 2–3 minutes or until the mixture is smooth.

2 Pour the mixture through a nut bag suspended over a jug, pitcher or bowl and leave to drain. If you don't have a nut bag, use a muslin-lined sieve.

3 When the milk has filtered through, gather up the corners of the nut bag or muslin and gently squeeze with clean hands to extract the last few drops of milk.

4 Discard any bits of seed remaining in the nut bag or muslin (there should be very few). Store the milk, covered, in the refrigerator and use within 3 days.

Oat milk

Home-made oat milk is simple and cheap to make, but has a somewhat bland flavour. It will also separate quickly unless you add an emulsifier such as lecithin.

90g/3½oz/1 cup rolled oats
750ml/1¼ pints/3 cups filtered water,
  plus soaking water
pinch of sea salt (optional)
5ml/1 tsp agave syrup or clear honey (optional)
2.5ml/½ tsp vanilla extract (optional)
15ml/1 tbsp powdered lecithin (optional)

Makes about 800ml/1 pint 7fl oz/3¼ cups

1 Put the oats in a bowl with enough cold water to cover by 2.5cm/1in. Leave to soak for 15 minutes, then drain and rinse under cold running water (this is essential or the milk will have a slimy texture). Drain.

2 Put the oats and water in a blender; leave to soak for 5 minutes. Blend for 2 minutes, until smooth, then pour through a very fine sieve or one lined with muslin, into a bowl, jug or pitcher. Gently stir.

3 If using a flavouring, sweeteners or emulsifier, return the milk to the rinsed-out blender, add the ingredients and blend for 1 minute. Store, chilled, for up to 5 days. It will thicken, so stir it well before using.

MAKING COCONUT MILK AND COCONUT PRODUCTS

Coconut milk is made by soaking coconut flesh with hot water, then cooling and squeezing the resulting liquid through a fine sieve (strainer) to remove the solids. It has a rich, creamy taste and a colour and appearance similar to that of cow's milk due to its naturally high fat content. Coconut cream is the thick part of the milk that rises to the top. Creamed coconut is a solid block that can be melted into dishes when cooking or used to make coconut milk.

COCONUT MILK AND COCONUT CREAM

You can buy two types of coconut milk: 'thick' coconut milk, which is made by directly squeezing grated coconut flesh through muslin (cheesecloth), and 'thin' coconut milk, whereby the already-squeezed flesh is then soaked in hot water for a second and third time before being strained. You can use real coconut water, though it isn't typical. The method below can be used for making both types of coconut milk as well as coconut cream, all of which are very versatile dairy-free ingredients. The leftover pulp can also be used to make coconut flour.

1 Remove the flesh from a mature coconut (see the box opposite) and peel away the brown skin. Chop the flesh into pieces and place in a food processor. Pour over 150ml/ ¼ pint/⅔ cup near-boiling water. Blend until fairly smooth, then leave to cool for 5 minutes and blend again for just a few seconds.

2 Pour the mixture into a sieve lined with muslin or a clean dish towel over a glass, china or plastic bowl (coconut reacts with metal) and leave it to drain. Bring the corners of the muslin or dish towel together, then squeeze to extract the milk.

3 Set aside the liquid for about 30 minutes. The coconut cream will float to the top of the milk and can be spooned off the surface. This process of soaking and squeezing can be repeated to make more (slightly thinner) coconut milk. Don't discard the coconut pulp; it can be used to make coconut flour (see pages 38–9). One coconut will yield about 250ml/9fl oz/1 cup coconut milk and cream.

CREAMED COCONUT

Sold as a small solid block, creamed coconut is the ground, unsweetened, dehydrated flesh of a mature coconut that has been blended to a paste then compressed. Not to be confused with coconut cream, which is a concentrated liquid, creamed coconut has an intense flavour and can be stored at room temperature. To use, it can be grated or chopped and will melt in the heat of a dish. Stirred into hot water it can be made into coconut milk, but not cream. Sachets of creamed coconut are also available, typically containing 50g/2oz. To prepare, immerse the unopened sachet in very hot water, until the creamed coconut is melted.

Whipped coconut cream

This low-fat alternative to dairy whipped cream is very rich, so serve in small helpings. This method does not work as well with canned coconut cream, so use the cream spooned from the top of coconut milk, as outlined below.

400ml/14oz can full-fat coconut milk, chilled overnight
5ml/1 tsp vanilla extract

Makes about 150ml/¼ pint/⅔ cup

1 Chill the coconut milk in the refrigerator for several hours or overnight. Carefully open the can; the coconut cream will be at the top. Spoon out the coconut cream and place it in a glass bowl, preferably chilled, keeping the more watery coconut milk for other recipes.

2 Add the vanilla extract, then whisk for a few minutes with an electric beater, until the mixture is light and soft peaks form.

3 Serve the cream immediately or store it in the bowl, covered with clear film (plastic wrap) in the refrigerator. It will keep for 2–3 days.

Cook's tip

Whipped coconut cream is smoother in texture than nut creams, so may be preferable for some desserts, such as coconut, almond and raspberry-filled roll. It makes a great alternative to dairy cream to accompany fresh berries.

Preparing a mature coconut

Opening a mature coconut can be tricky, so take great care when breaking into the shell and make sure you have plenty of space.

1 Strip off some of the hairy husk from the coconut if necessary, then put the coconut in a preheated oven at 180°C/350°F/Gas 4 for 15 minutes. Remove from the oven and leave until cool enough to handle.

2 To extract the coconut water, put the coconut in a bowl that will firmly hold it upright. Use a clean drill bit, screwdriver or knife to carefully pierce holes in two of the 'eyes' on the top of the coconut. Turn the coconut upside down and allow the water to drain into the bowl below. You may need to strain it before use.

3 Nestle the coconut in a thick towel to hold it steady, and firmly strike around its circumference with the back (not the blade) of a heavy knife or cleaver, until the coconut cracks open. Alternatively, place the coconut in a strong, clean, plastic bag, take it outside and hit it with a hammer around the circumference.

4 Use a blunt, strong cutlery knife to prise the flesh from the shell, gouging in a direction away from your hand. You can then use a vegetable peeler to remove the brown skin from the white flesh.

BLENDING, FLAVOURING AND USING MILKS

Nut and seed milks are great for drinking and can be blended or flavoured with a wide range of other ingredients. They can also be used in cooking instead of dairy milk, or to make dairy-free yogurt and a cheese substitute. An excellent flour can be created from the nut or seed pulp left over from straining the milk.

BLENDING MILKS

Combinations of nuts and seeds can be soaked together, following the timings of whichever type needs the longest soaking and calculating the amount of water needed depending on the proportions of nuts or seeds; it's better to use slightly less water, then dilute the milk if necessary. There are several reasons you may choose to blend different nuts or seeds together:

1 To create a milk with a wider range of vitamins, minerals and other minerals, such as blending walnuts, rich in vitamin E, with Brazil nuts, an excellent source of selenium.

2 You may want to mix a more strongly flavoured milk, such as hemp milk, with a milder one, such as sunflower seed milk.

▼ Inexpensive oat milk can be blended with nut milks.

3 Some types of milk work together well: a blend of Brazil nut and coconut milk is lovely in tropical-fruit smoothies, and macadamia nut milk will add richness and creaminess to milder ones, such as sunflower seed milk.

4 To make nut milk go further, blend it with some oat milk (almond and oat is a popular combination) or add inexpensive peanut milk. To make peanut milk, substitute an equivalent weight of unroasted, unsalted and skinned peanuts for cashew nuts in the recipe on pages 20–1, soaking the peanuts for 6–8 hours.

FLAVOURING MILKS

All sorts of flavours can be used to create your favourite milk blends. Some can be added and soaked at the same time as the nuts; others need to be added to the made milk.

Cacao or cocoa powder These complement all milks, but go especially well with hazelnut milk. Cacao and unsweetened cocoa powder are different names for the same thing, but cacao powder specifically refers to unsweetened powder made at a low temperature. Add 10–15ml/2 tsp–1 tbsp cacao or cocoa powder to every 250ml/8fl oz/1 cup nut or seed milk before or after blending, along with some vanilla extract, if liked. Sweeten to taste.

Carob powder This is made by grinding the roasted pods of the evergreen carob tree. The pods contain a very sweet pulp and hard brown seeds. Carob has a similar taste to chocolate but is free from caffeine and has around half the fat of cocoa. It should be used in the same quantity as cacao or cocoa powder, but because it is slightly sweeter, you should add less sugar or sweetener to the blend.

Fresh fruit juices These can be used instead of filtered water when making nut milk. You could try apple juice with almonds; pear or cranberry juice with walnuts; and orange or pomegranate juice with cashew or Brazil nuts.

Dried fruits Soak these with the nuts to extract maximum flavour. Dried apricots and peaches work well with almond milk, while dried tropical fruits, such as pineapple, are good with Brazil nut or coconut milk. Little or no additional sweetener will be required.

Spices Warm spices such as cinnamon and ginger add a lovely aroma and flavour to nut or seed milks, and turmeric is renowned for its

▲ **Above left** Cacao powder and unsweetened cocoa add an intense chocolate flavour. **Above right** Dried apricots lend sweetness and flavour to milks.

anti-inflammatory properties. Add around 2.5ml/½ tsp ground spice to every 750ml/ 1¼ pints/3 cups milk. Alternatively, add chopped fresh stem ginger or some chopped preserved ginger from a jar along with a little of its syrup to the blender. Leave the milk to stand for a few minutes to let the spices infuse before straining. You will need to sweeten the milk to round out the flavour of the spices.

SUPERFOOD BLENDS
Each of the following can be added to 250ml/8fl oz/1 cup nut or seed milk:

- **Goji berries** Add 30ml/2 tbsp dried berries to the nut milk, leave to soak for 2–3 minutes, then blend until smooth. Also known as wolfberries, these berries are high in vitamin A and boost the immune system. They also promote a healthy heart and circulation.

- **Açai berries** Add 5ml/1 tsp açai berry powder to the nut milk and blend for 1 minute. These are rich in antioxidants and may help to promote weight loss.

- **Chia seeds** Sprinkle the little black seeds over the milk and pulse in the blender a few times. Leave for 3–5 minutes, then blend for about 5 seconds. These tiny mucilaginous (moist and sticky) seeds contribute omega-3 and omega-6 to the diet in the optimum ratio needed for a healthy heart and brain.

Vanilla This aromatic flavouring works well with all nut and seed milks. Add a few drops to enhance milks or, for a more pronounced taste, add 5–10ml/1–2 tsp vanilla extract or 1.5ml/ ¼ tsp pure ground vanilla bean paste to 750ml/ 1¼ pints/3 cups milk. This should be done after straining the milk, but if you don't want to see the little black specks of vanilla, blend the paste with the nuts and leave to stand for a few minutes before straining the milk.

Salt A tiny pinch of salt can balance the flavourings in nut and seed milks and bring out the natural taste. It can be added when soaking the nuts or when blending. Leave it out if you have high blood pressure or need to watch the sodium content of your diet.

▲ **Above left** Dates add sweetness and thicken milk. **Above middle** Coconut palm sugar has a low GI. **Above right** Honey is available in a range of different flavours.

SWEETENING MILKS

Most of the nut and seed milk recipes in this book are unsweetened, so can be used in savoury and sweet dishes, but when drinking, you may prefer a slightly sweeter taste. You can use a range of natural ingredients to do this, or ordinary caster (superfine) or soft light or dark brown sugar, which dissolve quickly and easily in the milk. Bear in mind that dark-coloured sweeteners will alter the colour of the milk. Try to buy organic versions and use sparingly: 5–10ml/1–2 tsp is usually enough to sweeten 800ml/1 pint 7fl oz/3¼ cups milk.

Agave syrup Sometimes labelled 'agave nectar', this gold-coloured syrup has a low Glycaemic Index (GI) and is a natural fructose sweetener extracted from the agave plant.

Coconut palm sugar and syrup Sometimes labelled 'coconut palm sugar' or 'crystallized coconut nectar', coconut sugar is subtly sweet and similar to brown sugar in appearance and taste but with a hint of caramel. It has a low GI and a high mineral content and comes as sugar crystals, or in block or liquid form. Coconut sugar is produced from the sap of flower buds and blossoms, which are boiled to make a thick syrup. The syrup can be further dried to make a block of sugar or crystals.

Dates These are a popular sweetener in nut milks as they add natural sweetness and help to thicken and stabilize the milk. They also contain an impressive concentration of nutrients, including potassium and the B-group of vitamins. Soft Medjool dates are particularly good (remember to check and remove the stones (pits) before adding). If using dried dates, add them to the bowl of soaking nuts for the last 30 minutes. Use two to three dates to sweeten 800ml/1 pint 7fl oz/3¼ cups of milk.

Honey This comes in a range of flavours, colours and thicknesses depending on the source and season. For most nut and seed milks a clear blended honey is a good choice. More neutral milks, such as cashew nut milk, may benefit from more intensively-flavoured honey such as heather, lavender or manuka.

Maple syrup The boiled-down sap of the North-American maple tree, this has a smooth, rich flavour and a reddish-brown colour. Cheaper versions are blended with corn syrup or carob fruit syrup so check labels carefully.

Stevia This is a calorie-free sugar substitute and comes as a white powder or granules. Made from the leaves of the stevia plant, it is about 30 times sweeter than sugar. Use in tiny amounts or it may have a slightly bitter aftertaste.

MAKING DAIRY-FREE INGREDIENTS
Nut milk yogurt and cheese substitute can be enjoyed in their own right or used in numerous recipes that contain their dairy counterparts.

Nut milk yogurt
This yogurt will not naturally thicken like dairy yogurt, so here nut milk is first thickened with cornflour (cornstarch). A little sugar, agave or maple syrup is essential as the probiotics 'feed' on this; the sweet taste will disappear by the end of the process. Don't substitute honey as it is antibacterial and may destroy the probiotics. Sweeten or flavour the yogurt *after* making it.

10ml/2 tsp cornflour (cornstarch)
7.5ml/1½ tsp caster (superfine) sugar, agave or maple syrup
475ml/16fl oz/2 cups freshly-made nut milk
two vegan probiotic capsules (acidophilus 40mg) or
  1 sachet non-dairy yogurt starter

Makes about 475ml/16fl oz/2 cups

1 Blend the cornflour and sugar, agave or maple syrup in a pan with 30ml/2 tbsp of the milk until smooth, then stir in the rest of the milk. Bring to the boil and simmer for 1 minute, whisking until the mixture is slightly thickened. Turn off the heat and leave to cool (you can speed up this process by placing the pan in a bowl of cold water) until the temperature falls to 90°F/32°C on a thermometer. Stir the mixture occasionally as it cools.

2 Open the probiotic capsules and sprinkle the powder over the warm milk (or add the sachet of yogurt starter, following the instructions on the packet) and whisk well.

3 Pour the mixture into a yogurt maker or a sterilized and cooled flask. Leave it to stand for 8–10 hours; after 8 hours the yogurt will have a mild flavour, so if you prefer it a little more tangy, leave it a little longer. Transfer it from the flask to a bowl and chill it, covered, in the refrigerator; it will thicken further as it chills. Use within 3 days of making.

4 For thicker yogurt, strain it after chilling it. Line a plastic or stainless-steel sieve (strainer), large enough to hold all the yogurt, with a piece of muslin (cheesecloth) and place it over a bowl. Tip the yogurt into the muslin and leave it to drain for 1–2 hours. The thin liquid will drain away, leaving a thicker yogurt behind in the muslin. Discard the liquid and tip the yogurt into the bowl. Cover and chill until needed.

Almond milk cheese

This mild, creamy cheese is made in the same way as almond milk, but here the pulp is used as a base for the cheese. Much less water is required when blending the almonds and some of the very creamy nut milk is left in the pulp. When freshly made, the cheese will have quite a sharp lemony flavour; this mellows and almost disappears after 24 hours.

175g/6oz/1 cup raw unsalted blanched almonds
175ml/6fl oz/¾ cup filtered water, plus water for soaking
45ml/3 tbsp freshly-squeezed lemon juice
45ml/3 tbsp olive oil
salt and ground white pepper, to taste

Makes 1 x 375g/13oz almond cheese

1 Put the almonds in a bowl and pour over enough water to cover by 2.5cm/1in. Leave to soak at room temperature for 2 hours, then drain and rinse. Return the nuts to the bowl, pour over the filtered water, cover and leave to soak in the refrigerator for 24 hours.

2 Tip the nuts and water into a food processor or blender (it's important that the mixture covers the blades or it will be impossible to blend it finely enough). Pulse a few times to break up the nuts, then blend continuously for 3–4 minutes, until very smooth. Tip the mixture into a nut bag suspended over a bowl and leave to drain for 5 minutes; the pulp should still be fairly moist. Transfer to a separate bowl.

3 Whisk the lemon juice with the olive oil, salt and pepper. Stir into the nut pulp. The mixture ought to be soft, but you should be able to shape it. If it is dry, stir in a little of the milk that has drained from the pulp. The remaining milk can be diluted and used separately.

4 Shape into a flattened round about 5cm/2in high and place on a baking sheet lined with baking parchment. Place in a cold oven and heat to 150°C/300°F/Gas 2. Bake for 25–30 minutes or until the outside is dry and slightly darker; this forms a 'rind' that will keep the cheese fresh. Leave to cool on the baking sheet, then transfer to a plate, cover and chill for 24 hours before serving. Eat within 5 days.

NUT FLOUR

After straining nut milks, there will be some damp leftover pulp in the nut bag or muslin; the amount will depend on the type of nut used and how finely you have ground them. This can be dried and made into nut 'flour'.

Nut flour is gluten-free and contains a higher amount of fibre than ordinary flour; measured by volume, it also weighs a lot less. As it is low in digestible carbohydrates it has a small impact on blood-sugar levels, so is ideal for those watching their carbohydrate intake, diabetics and pre-diabetics. It is also suitable for coeliacs. Nut flour is not the same as ground nuts, although small amounts can be used as a substitute. Unlike pure ground nuts, the dried pulp will be low in fat, with a mild nutty flavour.

Making nut flour

Some nuts make better flour than others; blanched almonds, cashew nuts and macadamia nuts all make excellent flour that is virtually white in colour. The pulp from unskinned almonds and from hazelnuts can also be used for making flour, although it will be darker in colour (flour from unskinned almonds will be speckled). You can also make coconut flour using this method.

1 Preheat the oven to 110°C/220°F/Gas ¼. Line a baking sheet with baking parchment (don't use foil). Spread the leftover pulp from making nut milk over the baking parchment in a thin, even layer, using a fork to break up the larger lumps.

2 Bake the nut pulp for 15 minutes, then remove the sheet from the oven and stir the pulp with a fork. Spread it out again into an even layer and bake it for a further 10–15 minutes or until it is completely dry. It can burn even at a very low temperature, so check it often towards the end of the cooking time.

3 Remove the baking sheet from the oven and leave until the dried pulp is completely cool. Tip it into a food processor and process for 3–4 minutes or until it is very finely ground. Store the nut flour in an airtight container at room temperature for a few weeks, in the refrigerator for up to 2 months, or in the freezer for up to 6 months.

Ways to use nut flour

- Substitute 25g/1oz/¼ cup nut flour in every 115g/4oz/1 cup plain (all-purpose) flour when making cakes and pastry. You can use a higher proportion in cookies, some cakes and muffins; they will have a denser and chewier texture.

- Replace some or all of the flour when making crumbles. Almond flour is lovely with fruit such as peaches and apricots, while hazelnut flour is especially good with apples, pears and plums.

- Nut flour makes a great gluten-free coating for egg-dipped strips of chicken and fish, and bakes or fries to form a crispy crust.

- Coconut flour has a distinctive coconut flavour. It absorbs a huge amount of liquid, so when baking add at least the equivalent amount of liquid to the amount of coconut flour. Because it is gluten-free, you will also need to use extra binding ingredients such as eggs, or sweeteners such as honey or maple syrup. Either use baking recipes that have been specially developed using coconut flour, or substitute 10–30 per cent of grain-based flours with coconut flour and add more egg and liquid to bind. It can also be used to thicken sauces and gravies.

MAKING NUT BUTTERS

Commercial nut butters usually contain added sugars, salt and preservatives; home-made ones are generally healthier. In addition, you can make them smooth, crunchy or somewhere in between the two consistencies. Most nut butters are made with just a single variety of nut, but once you have mastered the basic method you can make them with any combination of your favourite types. If you have a powerful food processor or blender you can make nut butter just with nuts. If you have a less powerful food processor or prefer a softer consistency, you should add a tiny amount of oil, such as groundnut oil, or any neutral-flavoured oil, such as sunflower oil.

PEANUT BUTTER

Packed with protein and flavour, peanut butter is a breakfast staple in many countries and it remains as popular today as it was when it was first produced. Whether you prefer it smooth or crunchy, it is very easy to make yourself.

Smooth peanut butter

This is the simplest peanut butter, which is blended until smooth and made with unroasted, unsalted nuts; ideal if you are following a 'raw' diet. It has a lighter colour and milder flavour than commercial peanut butter. If you wish to sweeten it, you can use brown sugar or, for softer nut butter, add a liquid sweetener such as honey, agave or maple syrup.

450g/1lb/2¾ cups raw unsalted peanuts
1.5ml/¼ tsp salt (optional)
5–10ml/1–2 tsp clear honey, agave or maple syrup (optional)
5–10ml/1–2 tsp groundnut (peanut) or sunflower oil (optional)

Makes about 450g/1lb/2 cups

1 Put the peanuts in a food processor or blender. Sprinkle with salt if you are using it. Pulse the blender a few times to start breaking up the nuts, then process for 1 minute or until the peanuts are finely ground.

2 Scrape the sides of the bowl with a rubber spatula, then add the sugar or sweetener, if using, and 5ml/1 tsp of the oil if you don't have a high-powered blender or food processor; this will help to soften the nuts so that they blend smoothly. Process the mixture for 2–3 minutes, until the nuts come together in a clumpy paste. Stop and scrape down the sides of the bowl again. Take care not to overheat the machine; stop if necessary.

3 Continue processing the mixture for a further 2–3 minutes; at first the peanut butter will get thicker, but gradually it will become smoother and creamier as it begins to flow freely through the blades. Add the remaining oil at this stage, if using.

▲ Silky-smooth peanut butter is a popular treat.

4 Blend for an additional 1 minute, or until the desired consistency is reached; the motor of the food processor or blender will warm the mixture slightly, so bear in mind that it will be slightly thicker when it has cooled.

5 Use a rubber spatula to transfer the peanut butter into a clean container or sterilized jars.

6 Store the peanut butter in the refrigerator (home-made nut butter doesn't contain preservatives, so it won't keep as long as commercial varieties). Use within 4 weeks of making. For longer storage, decant it into suitable freezerproof containers and freeze for up to 3 months.

SKINNING AND ROASTING PEANUTS

You can often buy raw unsalted peanuts with their skins removed, but some stores only sell those in their reddish-brown papery skins. You can of course leave the skins on when making peanut butter (they will add fibre and red flecks to the nut butter), but if you want to remove them there are two easy ways:

1 Heat the oven to 180°C/350°F/Gas 4. Spread the peanuts in a single layer on a baking sheet. Bake for 3–4 minutes or until the skins start to split away from the nuts (if you want to roast the nuts at the same time, cook them for a further 2–3 minutes. This will intesify the flavour). Put the hot nuts in a clean dish towel and rub vigorously to remove the skins. Pick out the skinned nuts and shake the skins off the dish towel into a bin.

2 If you don't want to cook the nuts, put them in the freezer for at least 4 hours or overnight in you prefer. Take out a large handful of nuts at a time and rub them vigorously in a clean dish towel. Most of the skins will be dislodged. You can remove the skinned nuts. Repeat until all the nuts are skinned.

Crunchy peanut butter

Here the peanuts are roasted until golden before being turned into peanut butter. Roasting the nuts intensifies the flavour and will make a darker, richer peanut butter. It also warms and helps release the natural oils, so this nut butter is quicker and easier to make than one made with unroasted nuts.

450g/1lb/2¾ cups raw unsalted peanuts
1.5ml/¼ tsp salt (optional)
5–10ml/1–2 tsp clear honey, agave or maple syrup
   (optional)
5–10ml/1–2 tsp groundnut (peanut) or sunflower oil
   (optional)

Makes about 450g/1lb/2 cups

1 Heat the oven to 180°C/350°F/Gas 4. Spread out the raw peanuts in a single layer on a baking sheet. Bake for 5–6 minutes; the nuts should be a light-golden colour and smell slightly nutty. Watch them carefully as nuts burn easily and over-roasting will make them taste bitter.

2 Remove from the oven, then leave the nuts on the baking sheet for 2–3 minutes. Set aside about 115g/4oz/¾ cup of the roasted nuts, then tip the rest into the food processor or blender. Sprinkle with salt, if you are using some. Pulse the blender a few times to start breaking up the nuts, then process the peanuts for 1 minute or until finely ground.

3 Scrape the sides of the bowl with a rubber spatula, then add the honey, agave or maple syrup, if using, and 5ml/1 tsp of the oil if you do not have a high-powered blender or food processor. Blend for 1–2 minutes or until the nuts come together in a clumpy paste. Stop and scrape down the sides of the bowl again.

4 Continue processing for 1–2 minutes more, until the peanut butter starts to become softer and creamier. Add the remaining oil at this stage, if using. Blend for an additional 1 minute or until smooth. Add the remaining nuts, then pulse until they are roughly chopped (if you want the pieces to be very even, chop the nuts by hand and then stir them into the butter). Transfer the peanut butter to a clean container or sterilized jars. Store in a cool place, preferably in the refrigerator, and use within 4 weeks of making, or freeze for up to 3 months.

OTHER NUT BUTTERS

While peanut butter may be the first nut butter that comes to mind, all kinds of shelled nuts can easily be made into nut butters. The length of time it takes to blend the nut butter and the final texture depends on the type of machine you own and on the oil content of the nuts. Be aware that the mixture is likely to heat up considerably while you are processing the nuts, so to avoid burns leave the butter in the food processor to cool before tasting or decanting it. Pause frequently if you are using a low-powered machine to prevent it from overheating.

Almond butter

An increasingly popular nut butter, almonds are very hard, so will take slightly longer to process than some other nuts. If you are making the butter in an ordinary food processor, it's a good idea to warm the almonds in the oven for a few minutes first to soften them and start releasing the oils (you can leave this step out if you are using a high-powered blender). If you make this nut butter with blanched almonds (see page 24) it will have a light, creamy colour, whereas using nuts with their skins on produces a darker, slightly speckled spread.

400g/14oz/2⅓ cups raw unsalted almonds
pinch of salt (optional)
5–10ml/1–2 tsp honey, agave or maple syrup (optional)
5–10ml/1–2 tsp almond or sunflower oil (optional)

Makes about 400g/14oz/scant 2 cups

1 Spread the almonds in a single layer on a baking sheet and put in a cold oven. Turn on the oven to 150°C/300°F/Gas 2. Heat for 4–5 minutes or until the almonds are warm.

2 Remove the almonds from the oven and tip them into the food processor. Sprinkle over the salt, if using. Process for 1–2 minutes, until finely ground. Scrape the sides with a rubber spatula, then add the sweetener and 5ml/1 tsp of the oil, if using. Blend for a few minutes or until the nuts come together in a clumpy paste. Stop and scrape down the sides again.

Almond chutney

Serve this with fried and grilled (broiled) snacks or use it as a dip with poppadums.

50g/2oz/½ cup raw unsalted blanched almonds
1 fresh green chilli, chopped (seeded if preferred)
1 small clove garlic
1cm/½in piece of fresh root ginger, chopped
15ml/1 tbsp fresh coriander (cilantro)
30ml/2 tbsp fresh mint leaves
2.5ml/½ tsp salt
5ml/1 tsp sugar
15ml/1 tbsp lemon juice

Makes about 75g/3oz/6 tbsp

1 Soak the almonds in 175ml/6fl oz/¾ cup boiling water for 20 minutes.

2 Transfer the nuts to a blender, with the water in which they were soaked. Add the remaining ingredients and blend until fairly smooth. Transfer to a bowl, cover with clear film (plastic wrap) and chill.

3 Add the remaining 5ml/1 tsp of oil, if using. Continue processing for 2–15 minutes, until smooth and creamy. The heat of the machine will help the nuts to soften and blend, but if using a low-powered one, take care not to burn out the engine; pause if necessary.

4 Transfer the butter to a clean container or sterilized jars. Store, chilled for up to 4 weeks.

Cashew nut butter

You can make cashew nut butter with raw unroasted nuts, but the flavour is much more intense if they are roasted first. Cashew nuts are much softer than either peanuts or almonds so this nut butter will blend more quickly and tends to have a much finer, smoother consistency than some home-made nut butters.

400g/14oz/2⅓ cups raw unsalted cashew nuts
pinch of salt (optional)
5–10ml/1–2 tsp honey, agave or maple syrup (optional)
5–10ml/1–2 tsp almond or sunflower oil (optional)

Makes about 400g/14oz/scant 2 cups

1 Preheat the oven to180°C/350°F/Gas 4. Spread the cashew nuts in a single layer on a baking sheet and roast for 5–6 minutes or until light golden. Take care not to let them burn.

2 Remove from the oven and leave the nuts to cool on the baking sheet for 2–3 minutes (very hot nuts could damage your machine), then tip them into the food processor. Sprinkle over the salt, if using. Process for 1–2 minutes or until finely ground.

3 Scrape the sides of the bowl with a rubber spatula, then add the sweetener and 5ml/1 tsp of the oil, if using. Blend for a few minutes, until the nuts come together in a clumpy paste. Stop and scrape down the sides of the bowl.

▲ Raw cashew nuts make a smooth, unctuous butter.

4 Add the remaining 5ml/1 tsp of oil, if using, and continue processing until smooth and creamy, scraping down the sides if necessary. Transfer the nut butter to a clean container or sterilized jars. Store in a cool place, preferably the refrigerator. Use within 4 weeks of making or freeze the butter in a suitable container for up to 3 months.

SMOOTH OR CRUNCHY?

Some nut butters will blend to a smooth texture; others, such as almond butter, tend to be a bit more textured. If you want a crunchy nut butter, remove some of the nuts from the food processor once they are coarsely or finely chopped (depending on your preference). Blend the rest into a smooth nut butter, then add the reserved chopped nuts and pulse the machine until the chopped nuts and butter are just combined, or stir them in by hand.

Hazelnut butter

Roasting brings out the distinctive flavour of hazelnuts and they make a delicious nut butter. You can roast them in the oven, but this will remove some of the moisture inside the nuts. Here, the nuts are quickly toasted in a frying pan to lightly brown the outsides, without drying the nuts. Ready-roasted skinned hazelnuts can be used instead.

400g/14oz/2⅓ cups raw unsalted hazelnuts,
    skinned or unskinned
pinch of salt (optional)
5–10ml/1–2 tsp light soft brown sugar, honey, agave or
    maple syrup (optional)
10–15ml/2 tsp–1 tbsp hazelnut or sunflower oil

Makes about 400g/14oz/scant 2 cups

1 Put the hazelnuts in a single layer in a non-stick frying pan. Toast over a low heat for 4–5 minutes, stirring often. Remove from the heat as soon as they start to turn golden and smell nutty; they will continue to cook in the pan.

2 If the hazelnuts are still in their papery skins, tip them into a clean dish towel and rub them to remove most of the skins. Pick out the nuts and put them in a food processor or blender.

3 Sprinkle over the salt, if using. Process for 1–2 minutes or until finely ground. Scrape the sides with a rubber spatula, then add the sugar or sweetener and 5ml/1 tsp oil, if using.

PISTACHIO AND MACADAMIA NUT BUTTERS

These luxurious and expensive nuts can be made into butters in exactly the same way as almond butter, but be aware that the cost of making them will be high. Both are soft nuts, so will blend into butters quickly and easily. Macadamia nuts are very high in fat and the resulting butter will be very soft, so don't add any additional oil or liquid sweeteners when blending.

4 Blend for a few minutes or until the nuts come together in a clumpy paste. Scrape down the sides of the bowl again with the spatula. Add the remaining oil, if using, and continue processing until the hazelnut butter becomes fairly smooth and creamy. Transfer the butter to a clean container or sterilized jars. Store in a cool place, preferably in the refrigerator. Use within 4 weeks of making or freeze in a suitable container for up to 3 months.

Chocolate hazelnut spread

Hazelnuts and chocolate have a natural affinity and it's not only children who adore this rich, nutty spread. This version contains a much higher proportion of nuts than commercial varieties and doesn't contain hydrogenated oils or thickeners. Use a good-quality chocolate but one that is not too high in cocoa solids; it should have a slightly sweet flavour. Unrefined icing (confectioners') sugar adds a hint of caramel but you can use white icing sugar if you prefer. For a sweeter version, omit the cocoa powder.

350g/12oz plain (semi-sweet) chocolate
175g/6oz/1 cup raw unsalted hazelnuts
pinch of salt
30ml/2 tbsp hazelnut oil or sunflower oil
45ml/3 tbsp unrefined icing (confectioners') sugar
15ml/1 tbsp unsweetened cocoa powder
2.5ml/½ tsp vanilla extract

Makes about 575g/1lb 7oz/2½ cups

1 Break the chocolate into squares and melt it in a bowl set over a pan of near-boiling water, stirring occasionally. Remove and leave to cool.

2 Toast and skin the hazelnuts, following steps 1 and 2 of hazelnut butter (page 45). Sprinkle over the salt. Process for 1–2 minutes, until the nuts are finely ground. Scrape the sides with a rubber spatula. Add the oil, then blend until the nuts come together in a fairly smooth nut butter, scraping the sides occasionally.

USING CHOCOLATE HAZELNUT SPREAD

- Add some chocolate hazelnut spread to milkshakes or smoothies. Try 15ml/1 tbsp blended with 1 small ripe banana and 250ml/8fl oz/1 cup nut milk.

- Use it as a filling to sandwich cookies or macarons together.

- Add a surprise centre to cupcakes: spoon half the cake mixture into the cake cases, add 2.5ml/½ tsp chocolate hazelnut spread to each, then top with the rest of the mixture before baking.

- Use it to flavour sauces and custards. Stir 30ml/2 tbsp into 300ml/½ pint/1¼ cups hot walnut milk custard (see page 107).

- Make it into truffles. Chill the chocolate hazelnut spread, then scoop out small teaspoonfuls. Shape into balls and dip into melted chocolate. Leave these to set on a sheet of baking parchment.

3 Add the oil, sugar, cocoa powder and vanilla and continue processing until the mixture is smooth. Add the chocolate and blend well.

4 Transfer to a clean container or sterilized jars. The mixture will be thin initially, but will thicken as it cools. Store at room temperature or, if you prefer it very thick, keep it in the refrigerator. Use within 3 weeks.

Chestnut butter

Making a butter from chestnuts is completely different to making one from any other nuts as they have a high carbohydrate and low fat content.

250g/9oz/1½ cups cooked and peeled chestnuts
30ml/2 tbsp clear honey
pinch of salt
120–150ml/4–5fl oz/½–⅔ cup filtered water

Makes about 400g/14oz/scant 2 cups

1 Put the chestnuts in a food processor and pulse for 1–2 minutes to break them up. Add the honey and salt and blend for an additional few seconds to combine.

2 With the motor running, slowly add 120ml/4fl oz/ ½ cup of water. Blend for 1–2 minutes, then scrape down the sides. Blend until very smooth, adding a little more water if needed.

3 Spoon the chestnut butter into an airtight container or sterilized jars and seal. Keep the butter in the refrigerator and use it within 3 weeks of making it.

Cook's tip

If you buy whole unpeeled chestnuts, cook and peel them following the method on page 29. You will need 675g/1½lb unpeeled chestnuts to yield 450g/1lb peeled ones.

Coconut butter

Although coconut oil and coconut butter are different products, some manufacturers use the terms interchangeably. The oil is pure oil extracted from copra (dried matured coconut flesh); the butter is made by crushing and blending finely chopped copra. Coconut butter can be used as a spread and in baking, but should not be used for frying as it burns at a very low temperature. Sometimes the oil may separate and rise to the top, in which case give it a stir before using it.

250g/9oz/3 cups unsweetened full-fat desiccated
   (dry unsweetened shredded) coconut

Makes about 250g/9oz/2 cups

1 Process the desiccated coconut in a food processor for 3–4 minutes, then scrape down the sides. Blend again, stopping after several minutes and scraping down the sides again.

2 Keep repeating this procedure and blend until the mixture has become oily and a fairly smooth, pale paste. This can take 20 minutes.

3 Transfer the butter to a sterilized jar and store it at room temperature. It will keep for at least a year. If it sets hard (in a cold room), warm it for a few seconds in the microwave.

MAKING SEED BUTTERS

Like nuts, seeds are nutritional powerhouses and are easy to turn into thick and creamy butters. They can be spread on bread, used in baking or stirred into rice dishes at the end of the cooking time.

SUNFLOWER OR PUMPKIN SEED BUTTER

Sunflower seeds make a dark cream-coloured butter, whereas pumpkin seeds blend to a speckled olive-green. If you can't choose between the two types, use half of each to make a nutrient-rich spread.

300g/11oz/3 cups sunflower or pumpkin seeds
pinch of sea salt
15–30ml/1–2 tbsp sunflower or pumpkin seed oil
10ml/2 tsp maple syrup (optional)

Makes about 300g/11oz/1½ cups

1 Put the seeds in a large non-stick frying pan. Toast over a low heat for 5–6 minutes, shaking the pan and stirring the seeds frequently. They are ready when some are just starting to colour, they smell nutty and you hear a sizzling sound. Remove from the heat and stir for 1 minute.

2 Leave to cool, then tip into a food processor or blender. Add the sea salt and process for 1–2 minutes, until finely ground. Add 15ml/ 1 tbsp oil and the maple syrup if using, then process for 3–4 minutes.

▲ Sesame seeds are used to make two types of butter.

3 Scrape down the sides with a spatula and continue processing until the butter becomes fairly smooth and creamy. Add a little more or all of the oil, if liked, to make a thinner butter.

4 Transfer to a clean container or sterilized jars. Store in a cool place, preferably in the refrigerator. Use within 4 weeks or freeze in a suitable container for up to 3 months.

SESAME SEED BUTTERS

There are two types of sesame seed butter. Tahini is a smooth, thick paste made from unroasted sesame seeds and usually contains olive oil. It is a flavouring ingredient in Middle Eastern dishes such as hummus and baba ganoush. Toasted sesame seed butter is denser and deeper in taste and colour as the seeds are roasted. It is often used in stir-fries and sauces.

Tahini

Here the seeds are soaked to soften them and give the butter a smoother, creamier consistency. It will thicken as it cools.

150g/5oz/1 cup sesame seeds
pinch of salt
45–60ml/3–4 tbsp olive oil

Makes about 200g/7oz/1 cup

1 Put the seeds in a bowl and pour over enough cold filtered water to cover them by 2.5cm/1in (a lot will float on the top, but will sink as they absorb water). Leave to soak for 4–6 hours.

2 Drain the seeds in a fine sieve (strainer), then tip into a food processor. Add the salt and process for 1–2 minutes, until finely ground. Scrape down the sides and process again.

3 With the motor running, add 30ml/2 tbsp oil. Blend until smooth, add 15ml/1 tbsp more oil and blend again, adding more oil until you achieve the desired consistency.

4 Transfer to a bowl or sterilized jar. Cover and store in the refrigerator for up to 4 weeks. Some of the oil may float to the top, so stir before using.

Toasted sesame seed butter

For this butter, the seeds are lightly toasted in a frying pan. They brown very quickly, so watch carefully and stir continuously.

150g/5oz/1 cup sesame seeds
15–30ml/1–2 tbsp toasted sesame oil
pinch of salt

Makes about 175g/6oz/generous ¾ cup

1 Put the seeds in a non-stick frying pan. Toast over a low heat for 2–3 minutes, stirring constantly, until the seeds are just turning golden-brown. Remove from the heat and continue to stir for 1 minute.

2 Leave the seeds to cool for 1 minute, then tip them into a food processor. Add the oil and salt. Pulse for 2–3 minutes, until finely ground. Scrape down the sides with a spatula.

3 Continue blending until the mixture is fairly smooth, scraping down the sides. Add a little more oil if necessary to keep the mixture moving over the food processor's blades.

4 Transfer to a bowl or sterilized jar. Cover and store in the refrigerator for up to 4 weeks. Some of the oil may float to the top, so stir before using.

USING NUT AND SEED BUTTERS

Nut and seed butters are not only great for spreading on bread, but are a versatile cooking ingredient as well. They can be used to flavour sweet and savoury dishes, to thicken sauces and to replace dairy cream in many recipes.

NUT CREAMS

When cooking, the simplest nut creams can be made by blending nut butter with water or another liquid until smooth. When incorporating with other ingredients, a neutral-flavoured nut butter such as almond or cashew nut is ideal.

Simple nut cream

This nut cream can also be turned into a quick-and-easy sauce for pasta; walnut butter or pine nut butter are both perfect for this. Use the hot pasta water and add some chopped fresh herbs, a squeeze of lemon juice and some salt and ground black pepper to add a finishing flourish to the sauce.

115g/4oz/½ cup nut butter
up to 250ml/8fl oz/1 cup warm or hot water,
   stock or nut milk

Makes about 300g/11oz/1½ cups

1 Put the nut butter in a bowl. Stir in a few tablespoons of warm or hot water (you can use stock if you are making a savoury recipe or nut milk if you want a very rich mixture for a sweet recipe) and blend together until smooth.

2 Gradually work in more water or liquid; up to 250ml/8fl oz/1 cup will make a thick cream with a consistency of dairy double (heavy) cream. Add a little more liquid if you want a thinner cream. Use while the cream is still warm, or cool it before use.

WAYS TO USE NUT AND SEED BUTTERS

- **Coating** Mix nut or seed butter with a little extra oil, fresh herbs and seasoning then spread over thin cuts of meat, such as chicken breast fillets; rack of lamb; fish fillets or steaks; or thin slices of courgette (zucchini) or aubergine (eggplant). Oven-bake until the meat, fish or vegetable is tender and the nut or seed butter crust browned. Don't try this with meat, fish or starchy vegetables that require long cooking as the topping cooks quickly.

- **Stuffing** Nut or seed butters can be added to stuffing for vegetables, such as halved (bell) peppers, and meat such as pork fillet (tenderloin) and chicken breast fillets (make a pocket in the meat and spoon in a little nut or seed butter).

- **Pastry** Add a nutty flavour to pastry by using a little nut butter instead of some of the fat when making it (see page 91).

- **Thickening** Nut or seed butters are a great way to thicken gravies, soups and stews. Blend some sauce into 15ml/ 1 tbsp nut butter, then whisk the mixture back into the dish.

Cashew nut cream

Cashews are ideal for making thick nut creams as the soft nuts blend to a white product with a super-smooth consistency. This can be as thick as you like; the consistency of whipped cream or thinned with more liquid to make a pourable cream.

250g/9oz/2½ cups unsalted raw cashew nuts
250ml/8fl oz/1 cup filtered water,
   plus soaking water
icing (confectioners') sugar, agave or maple syrup,
   or lemon juice and ground black pepper

Makes about 500ml/17fl oz/generous 2 cups

1 Put the unsalted raw cashew nuts in a large glass, ceramic or stainless steel bowl. Pour over enough water to cover by about 2.5cm/1in and leave to soak for at least 8 hours, or overnight.

2 Drain and rinse the nuts, then tip into a blender. Pulse a few times. With the motor running, slowly pour in the water, stopping to scrape down the sides. Blend until smooth and creamy.

3 Add more water if you want a thinner consistency. For a sweet cream, add a little icing sugar, agave or maple syrup; for use in a savoury dish, add lemon juice and season with ground pepper.

Dairy-free pine nut pesto

This Genoese sauce often contains grated Parmesan cheese, but this version is dairy-free; the tangy taste of cheese replaced with fresh lemon juice and a generous amount of seasoning.

50g/2oz/½ cup pine nuts
50g/2oz fresh basil leaves
1–2 cloves garlic, peeled
120ml/4fl oz/½ cup extra-virgin olive oil
10–15ml/2 tsp–1 tbsp freshly squeezed lemon juice
salt and ground black pepper

Makes about 225ml/7½fl oz/scant 1 cup

1 Toast the pine nuts in a single layer in a non-stick frying pan over a low heat for 2–3 minutes, stirring, until just beginning to turn light golden. Tip the nuts on to a plate and leave until they are nearly cool.

2 Put the pine nuts, basil, garlic, olive oil, 10ml/2 tsp of the lemon juice, salt and pepper in a blender or food processor. Blend at high speed until the nuts and basil are finely chopped and the mixture is creamy.

3 Taste and adjust the seasoning as necessary, adding the remaining lemon juice if needed. Store in a screw-top jar in the refrigerator, spooning a little extra oil over the top. Use within 3 weeks.

RECIPES USING NUT AND SEED MILKS AND BUTTERS

Nut and seed milks and butters, along with other easy-to-make products such as cream, yogurt or cheese, can be used in a wide range of delicious everyday recipes, including smoothies, soups, snacks and salads as well as curries, casseroles and sweet treats. This section contains more than 70 dairy-free dishes that you can try at home, along with cook's tips and variations to help you achieve perfect results every time. From familiar classics, such as porridge, muffins and chicken satay, to more unusual treats, such as spicy walnut dip and almond milk couscous, there is a way to incorporate health-giving nuts and seeds in all your cooking!

◀ Nuts and seeds can be transformed into a wide range of milks and butters.

▼ Almond Milk and Blackberry Muffins.

BREAKFASTS AND DRINKS

ALMOND YOGURT WITH POMEGRANATE AND GRAPEFRUIT

Tart, sweet and juicy pomegranate seeds and segments of grapefruit, drizzled with honey and mixed with almond milk yogurt, are a refreshing way to start the day.

300ml/½ pint/1¼ cups almond milk yogurt
2–3 ripe pomegranates
bunch of mint, finely chopped
25ml/1½ tbsp clear honey
2 red grapefruits
2 pink grapefruits
1 white grapefruit
15ml/1 tbsp orange flower water

Serves 4

NUTRITIONAL INFORMATION:
Energy 191kcal/810kJ; Protein 3.4g; Carbohydrate 43g, of which sugars 34.7g; Fat 1.8g, of which saturates 0g; Cholesterol 0mg; Calcium 77mg; Fibre 8.6g; Sodium 34mg.

1 Beat the almond milk yogurt in a bowl. Cut open the pomegranates and scoop out the seeds, removing all the bitter pith. Fold most of the pomegranate and mint into the yogurt. Add the honey, then chill.

2 Peel all of the grapefruits, cutting off all the pith. Cut between the membranes to remove the segments, holding the fruit over a bowl to catch the juices.

3 Mix the fruit segments with the juices. Sprinkle with orange flower water and stir gently.

4 Divide the grapefruit among four plates. Top with the yogurt and scatter with the reserved pomegranate seeds and mint.

PORRIDGE WITH COCONUT MILK AND DATES

Full of valuable nutrients and fibre, puréed dates give a sweet flavour to this coconut porridge. Oats can help reduce blood-cholesterol levels as part of a healthy diet.

250g/9oz/scant 2 cups fresh dates
225g/8oz/2 cups rolled oats
750ml/1¼ pints/3 cups coconut milk
50g/2oz/½ cup raw unsalted pistachio nuts

Serves 4

NUTRITIONAL INFORMATION:
Energy 430kcal/1817kJ; Protein 10.3g; Carbohydrate 70.1g, of which sugars 29.1g; Fat 14.1g, of which saturates 2.6g; Cholesterol 0mg; Calcium 122mg; Fibre 7.3g; Sodium 230mg.

1 Halve the dates and remove the stones (pits) and stems. Cover with boiling water and soak for 30 minutes, until softened. Strain, reserving 90ml/6 tbsp of the soaking water.

2 Remove the skins from the dates and purée them in a food processor with the soaking water.

3 Place the oats in a pan with the coconut milk. Bring to the boil, reduce the heat and simmer for 4–5 minutes until cooked, stirring often. Serve topped with date purée and pistachio nuts.

COCONUT, SEED AND NUT GRANOLA WITH NUT YOGURT

Nuts, seeds, oats and dried fruits baked with honey and coconut oil make a nutritious breakfast. Serve with your favourite nut milk or yogurt and some fruit.

225g/8oz/2 cup rolled oats
50g/2oz/½ cup sunflower seeds
25g/1oz/2 tbsp sesame seeds
50g/2oz/½ cup hazelnuts, roasted
25g/1oz/¼ cup almonds, chopped
45ml/3 tbsp coconut oil
50ml/2fl oz/¼ cup clear honey
50g/2oz/½ cup raisins
50g/2oz/½ cup dried cranberries
nut milk or yogurt and fruit, to serve

Serves 4

NUTRITIONAL INFORMATION:
Energy 156kcal/657kJ; Protein 3.8g;
Carbohydrate 18.9g, of which sugars
6.9g; Fat 7.8g, of which saturates
2.4g; Cholesterol 0mg; Calcium
21.3mg; Fibre 2.2g; Sodium 9.3mg.

1 Preheat the oven to 140°C/ 275°F/Gas 1. Combine the oats, seeds and nuts.

2 Heat the coconut oil and honey in a large pan until melted, then remove from the heat.

3 Add the oat mixture to the pan and stir well. Spread out the mixture on one or two baking sheets.

4 Bake the mixture in the oven for about 50 minutes until crisp, stirring occasionally. Remove from the oven and mix in the raisins and cranberries.

5 Leave the granola to cool completely, then transfer it to an airtight container, breaking up larger pieces as you do so. Serve with some nut milk or nut yogurt and seasonal fresh fruit.

RASPBERRY AND HAZELNUT YOGURT CRANACHAN

Hazelnut milk yogurt is substituted for cream in this traditional Scottish recipe. Coconut, seed and nut granola can be used instead of oat cereal, if you prefer.

75g/3oz crunchy oat cereal
600ml/1 pint/2½ cups hazelnut
   milk yogurt
250g/9oz/1⅓ cups raspberries

Serves 4

NUTRITIONAL INFORMATION:
Energy 218kcal/927kJ; Protein 3.7g;
Carbohydrate 43.9g, of which sugars
18.8g; Fat 4.3g, of which saturates
0.4g; Cholesterol 0mg; Calcium
25mg; Fibre 7.5g; Sodium 59mg.

1 Gently fold the crunchy oat cereal into the hazelnut milk yogurt, taking care not to crush the cereal.

2 Reserve a few raspberries for the topping, then gently fold in the rest, taking care not to crush them.

3 Spoon the mixture into four glasses or dishes. Top with the remaining raspberries and serve immediately. You could drizzle over some clear honey if you like.

OAT AND PECAN NUT MILK PANCAKES WITH BANANAS

These healthy breakfast pancakes contain wholemeal flour and oats, and are more like American-style pancakes than classic thin French crêpes. Bananas and pecan nuts are gently cooked in maple syrup to make a sweet and delicious topping.

75g/3oz/⅔ cup plain (all-purpose) flour
50g/2oz/½ cup wholemeal
   (whole-wheat) flour
50g/2oz/½ cup rolled oats
5ml/1 tsp baking powder
pinch of salt
10ml/2 tsp caster (superfine) or
   coconut sugar
1 egg
250ml/8fl oz/1 cup pecan nut milk
15ml/1 tbsp sunflower oil,
   plus extra for frying

**FOR THE CARAMEL BANANAS
   AND PECAN NUTS**
15ml/1 tbsp coconut oil
15ml/1 tbsp maple syrup
3 bananas, halved lengthways
   and widthways
25g/1oz/¼ cup raw unsalted
   pecan nuts

Serves 5

Cook's tip
Pecan nuts are one of the richest sources of vitamin B6, which strengthens the immune system and helps release energy from food; a useful boost at the start of the day.

NUTRITIONAL INFORMATION:
Energy 303kcal/1277kJ; Protein 7.4g; Carbohydrate 45.1g, of which sugars 16.7g; Fat 11.7g, of which saturates 3.1g; Cholesterol 48mg; Calcium 55mg; Fibre 4.5g; Sodium 140mg.

1 To make the pancakes, mix together the plain and wholemeal flours, oats, baking powder, salt and sugar in a bowl. Make a well in the centre and add the egg and a quarter of the milk. Mix well, then gradually stir in the rest of the milk to make a thick batter. Leave to rest for 5 minutes at room temperature.

2 Heat a large, heavy, lightly oiled frying pan. Using 30ml/2 tbsp of batter for each pancake, cook two or three pancakes at a time. Cook for 3 minutes on each side or until golden. Keep warm while you cook the remaining pancakes.

3 To make the caramel bananas and pecan nuts, wipe out the frying pan and add the coconut oil. Heat gently until it is very liquid, then add the maple syrup and stir well. Add the bananas and pecan nuts to the pan.

4 Cook for about 4 minutes, turning once, or until the bananas have softened and the sauce has caramelized. To serve, place two pancakes on each warm plate and top with the caramel bananas and pecan nuts. Serve immediately.

ALMOND MILK MORNING ROLLS

Here, bread dough is allowed to slowly rise in the refrigerator overnight, ready to shape and bake in the morning. Almond milk adds flavour and softness to the rolls. They are delectable served warm, spread with coconut butter and topped with jam.

450g/1lb/4 cups unbleached
   strong white bread flour,
   plus extra for dusting
10ml/2 tsp salt
7g/¼oz easy-blend (rapid-rise)
   dried yeast
300ml/½ pint/1¼ cups cold
   almond milk

Makes 10

Variation
Crumble 20g/¾oz fresh yeast into a small bowl, then stir in about a quarter of the milk to make a smooth liquid. Stir in the rest of the milk and add to the flour and salt and mix as in step 1.

NUTRITIONAL INFORMATION:
Energy 157kcal/668kJ; Protein 4.4g; Carbohydrate 35.1g, of which sugars 0.7g; Fat 0.9g, of which saturates 0.1g; Cholesterol 0mg; Calcium 63mg; Fibre 2g; Sodium 414mg.

1 Sift the flour and salt into a bowl. Stir in the yeast. Make a well in the middle, pour in the almond milk and mix to a soft dough. Turn out on to a lightly floured surface and knead for 5–7 minutes, until the dough is smooth and elastic. Place the dough in a lightly oiled bowl and cover with clear film (plastic wrap). Leave in the refrigerator overnight to rise; it should double in size in 8–10 hours.

2 Take the dough out of the refrigerator and leave at room temperature for 30 minutes. Grease a large baking sheet.

3 Turn out the dough on to a lightly floured surface and gently knead for 1–2 minutes. Shape into 10 round or oval rolls and place on the baking sheet, spacing them slightly apart. Cover with oiled clear film and leave in a warm place for 30 minutes or until well-risen. Preheat the oven to 200°C/400°F/Gas 6.

4 Dust the top of the rolls with flour. Bake for 12–15 minutes, or until lightly browned. Remove from the oven and leave to cool slightly on a wire rack. Serve warm.

ALMOND MILK AND BLACKBERRY MUFFINS

These fruit-packed muffins help provide the energy boost the body needs to start the day. Fresh blackberries are used in this recipe, but you can substitute fresh or frozen blueberries if you prefer. You could also use different types of nut milk.

300g/11oz/2¾ cups plain
  (all-purpose) flour
50g/2oz/¼ cup soft light
  brown sugar
20ml/4 tsp baking powder
60g/2¼oz/½ cup raw unsalted
  blanched almonds, chopped
100g/3½oz/scant 1 cup fresh
  blackberries, rinsed and patted
  dry with kitchen paper
2 eggs
150ml/¼ pint/⅔ cup almond milk
45ml/3 tbsp sunflower oil
2.5ml/½ tsp vanilla extract

Makes 12

1 Preheat the oven to 200°C/400°F/Gas 6. Line the cups of a muffin tin (pan) with paper cases.

2 Sift the flour, sugar and baking powder into a large bowl. Stir in the almonds and blackberries, mixing them well to coat with the flour mixture. Make a well in the middle of the dry ingredients.

3 In another bowl, whisk the eggs with the almond milk, then mix in the oil and vanilla extract. Stir into the dry ingredients.

4 Spoon the batter into the prepared paper cases and bake for 20–25 minutes or until golden. Leave to stand for 5 minutes before turning out on to a wire rack to cool.

NUTRITIONAL INFORMATION: Energy 178kcal/750kJ; Protein 4.9g; Carbohydrate 25.3g, of which sugars 5.6g; Fat 7.1g, of which saturates 0.9g; Cholesterol 39mg; Calcium 72mg; Fibre 1.4g; Sodium 182mg.

FRUIT AND SEED BUTTER BREAKFAST BARS

These bars provide the perfect breakfast solution when time is short in the morning. No fat or oil needs to be added to the mixture as the blend of seed butter and apple sauce makes these nutty snacks beautifully moist.

45ml/3 tbsp sunflower or pumpkin seed butter
275g/10oz unsweetened apple sauce or purée
115g/4oz/½ cup ready-to-eat dried apricots, chopped
115g/4oz/¾ cup raisins
50g/2oz/¼ cup demerara (raw) sugar
30ml/2 tbsp sunflower seeds
30ml/2 tbsp sesame seeds
75g/3oz/scant 1 cup rolled oats
75g/3oz/⅔ cup self-raising (self-rising) wholemeal (whole-wheat) flour
50g/2oz/⅔ cup desiccated (dry unsweetened shredded) coconut
2 eggs, beaten

Makes 12

1 Preheat the oven to 200°C/400°F/Gas 6. Grease a 20cm/8in square shallow baking tin (pan) and line with baking parchment.

2 Put the seed butter in a bowl. Add 15ml/1 tbsp of the apple sauce and mix until blended, then add a few more spoonfuls, one at a time, blending well. When the mixture is quite loose, stir in the rest of the sauce. Add the apricots, raisins, sugar, sunflower seeds and sesame seeds and stir well.

3 Add the oats, flour, coconut and eggs to the fruit mixture and gently stir together until evenly combined. Turn the mixture into the tin and spread to the edges in an even layer.

4 Bake for about 20 minutes, or until golden and just firm to the touch. Leave to cool in the tin, then lift out on to a board and cut into bars.

NUTRITIONAL INFORMATION: Energy 214kcal/900kJ; Protein 5.2g; Carbohydrate 29.5g, of which sugars 19.9g; Fat 9g, of which saturates 3.2g; Cholesterol 39mg; Calcium 67mg; Fibre 3.7g; Sodium 53mg.

SMOKED COD OMELETTE WITH CASHEW NUT MILK

Whisked egg whites are folded into the smoked haddock mixture to make a soufflé-style omelette. This is best made with thick cashew nut milk for the creamiest flavour.

175g/6oz smoked cod fillet
4 eggs, separated
150ml/¼ pint/⅔ cup full-bodied
    cashew nut milk
ground black pepper
15ml/1 tbsp coconut or sunflower oil
watercress, to garnish

Serves 2

NUTRITIONAL INFORMATION:
Energy 348kcal/1446kJ; Protein 32.1g;
Carbohydrate 4.1g, of which sugars
2.2g; Fat 22.8g, of which saturates
9.3g; Cholesterol 502mg; Calcium
77mg; Fibre 0.3g; Sodium 1254mg.

1 Poach the cod in water to cover for 7–8 minutes, until just cooked. Drain, then remove the skin and any bones and flake the fish.

2 Mix the egg yolks with the cashew nut milk and season. Gently stir in the flaked fish.

3 Put the egg whites in a clean bowl and whisk until they form soft peaks. Fold the whites into the fish mixture.

4 Heat the oil in an omelette pan, add the mixture and cook gently for 3–4 minutes, until set and golden on the base. Place under a hot grill (broiler) for 1–2 minutes. Garnish and serve.

CHESTNUT MUSHROOMS ON TOAST

Chestnut mushrooms are slightly darker in colour and have a richer flavour than white ones. Chestnut milk makes a deliciously rich and tasty sauce.

250g/9oz chestnut mushrooms
15ml/1 tbsp sunflower oil
120ml/4fl oz/½ cup chestnut milk
salt and ground black pepper
pinch of freshly grated nutmeg
2 thick slices of toast
chopped chives, to garnish

Serves 2

NUTRITIONAL INFORMATION:
Energy 199kcal/838kJ; Protein 7.9g;
Carbohydrate 25.5g, of which sugars
1.7g; Fat 8.1g, of which saturates
1.2g; Cholesterol 0mg; Calcium
71mg; Fibre 3.2g; Sodium 286mg.

1 Pick over and trim the mushrooms, wipe them clean with kitchen paper if necessary, then cut them into thick slices.

2 Heat the oil in a non-stick pan, add the mushrooms and cook quickly for about 3 minutes, stirring frequently.

3 Tip the mushrooms into a bowl and set aside. Add the chestnut milk to the pan. Simmer for 4–5 minutes or until reduced by half. Add the mushrooms, season with salt, pepper and nutmeg and simmer for 2 minutes. Divide the mixture between the two pieces of toast, garnish with chopped chives and serve.

KEDGEREE WITH ALMOND MILK

The rice in this fragrant dish is simmered in almond milk, which gives it a nutty flavour. Excellent for breakfast or brunch, it could also be served as a light supper.

450g/1lb smoked haddock
300ml/½ pint/1¼ cups almond milk
175g/6oz/scant 1 cup long grain rice
salt and ground black pepper
pinch of freshly grated nutmeg
pinch of cayenne pepper
15ml/1 tbsp coconut or sunflower oil
1 onion, peeled and finely chopped
2 hard-boiled eggs
chopped fresh parsley, to garnish
lemon wedges and wholemeal
    (whole-wheat) toast, to serve

Serves 4–6

NUTRITIONAL INFORMATION:
Energy 227kcal/954kJ; Protein
19.4g; Carbohydrate 25.5g, of
which sugars 1.4g; Fat 5.2g, of
which saturates 0.9g; Cholesterol
104mg; Calcium 40mg; Fibre 0.8g;
Sodium 632mg.

1 Poach the haddock in the almond milk, made up with just enough water to cover the fish, for about 8 minutes, or until just cooked. Skin the haddock, remove all the bones and flake the flesh with a fork. Set aside.

2 Strain the almond milk poaching liquid into a measuring jug (cup) and make it up to 600ml/1 pint/2½ cups with water. Transfer the liquid to a pan, bring to the boil, add the rice, cover with a lid and cook over a low heat for 25 minutes, or until all the liquid has been absorbed by the rice. Turn off the heat. Season with salt, pepper, grated nutmeg and cayenne pepper.

3 Meanwhile, heat the coconut or vegetable oil in a pan, add the onion and fry until soft and transparent. Set aside. Roughly chop one of the eggs and slice the other into neat wedges.

4 Stir the flaked haddock, onion and the chopped egg into the rice. Heat the mixture through gently.

5 To serve, pile up the kedgeree on a warmed dish, garnish with parsley and arrange the wedges of egg on top. Put the lemon wedges around the base and serve hot with the toast.

BANANA, PINEAPPLE AND BRAZIL NUT MILK SHAKE

A 'breakfast in a glass', this smoothie contains pineapple and banana, blended with Brazil nut milk. Medjool dates add sweetness and make the mixture thicker.

½ pineapple
4 Medjool dates, stoned (pitted)
1 small ripe banana
juice of ½ lemon
300ml/½ pint/1¼ cups very cold
   Brazil nut milk

Serves 2–3

....
NUTRITIONAL INFORMATION:
Energy 208kcal/888kJ; Protein 2.6g;
Carbohydrate 49.7g, of which sugars
48.8g; Fat 1.6g, of which saturates
0.5g; Cholesterol 0mg; Calcium
44mg; Fibre 4.7g; Sodium 7mg.
....

1 Using a small, sharp knife, cut away the skin and core from the pineapple. Roughly chop the flesh and put it in a blender or food processor, then add the dates.

2 Peel and chop the banana and add it to the rest of the fruit with the lemon juice.

3 Blend until smooth, stopping to scrape the mixture down from the side of the bowl with a rubber spatula, if necessary. Add the Brazil nut milk and process briefly until well combined. Pour the smoothie into tall glasses and serve immediately.

PEAR, GINGER AND WALNUT MILK SHAKE

Although fresh fruit cannot be beaten for its flavour and nutritional value, canned varieties are a good alternative when the fresh type is unavailable.

3 pieces preserved stem ginger,
   plus 30ml/2 tbsp ginger syrup
   from the jar
400g/14oz can pears in natural
   fruit juice
450ml/¾ pint/scant 2 cups cold
   walnut milk
ice cubes

Serves 2

....
NUTRITIONAL INFORMATION:
Energy 299kcal/1262kJ; Protein 4.6g;
Carbohydrate 41.2g, of which sugars
32.2g; Fat 14.8g, of which saturates
1.9g; Cholesterol 9mg; Calcium
28mg; Fibre 5.9g; Sodium 158mg.
....

1 Shave off some wafer-thin slices from one of the pieces of ginger and set aside. Roughly chop the remaining ginger. Drain the pears, reserving about 150ml/¼ pint/ ⅔ cup of the juice.

2 Put the pears, measured juice and chopped ginger in a blender or food processor and blend until smooth, scraping the mixture down from the side of the bowl, if necessary.

3 Strain through a sieve (strainer) into a jug or pitcher. Whisk in the milk and ginger syrup and pour into two glasses. Serve with ice and top with the ginger shavings.

INDIAN-STYLE CASHEW NUT MILK AND MANGO DRINK

A luscious combination of mangoes, cashew nut milk and fragrant cardamom makes a refreshing fruit drink, packed with essential vitamins and minerals.

225g/8oz canned mango pulp or 425g/15oz can of sliced mangoes, drained
300ml/½ pint/1¼ cups cold cashew nut milk
5ml/1 tsp honey or sugar
2.5ml/½ tsp ground cardamom
sprigs of fresh mint, to garnish

Serves 4

NUTRITIONAL INFORMATION:
Energy 54kcal/230kJ; Protein 0.3g; Carbohydrate 13.4g, of which sugars 13.1g; Fat 0.3g, of which saturates 0.1g; Cholesterol 0mg; Calcium 6mg; Fibre 0.6g; Sodium 8mg.

1 Put the mango pulp or slices into a food processor and add the cashew nut milk, honey and cardamom.

2 Blend everything together until it is smooth, then transfer the mixture to a large jug or pitcher.

3 Add 300ml/½ pint/1¼ cups cold water. Mix well and chill in the refrigerator.

4 When you are ready to serve, pour the drink into four glasses. Serve the drink immediately, while it is still cold, garnished with the mint sprigs.

PAPAYA AND ALMOND YOGURT LASSI

This drink provides a nourishing start to the day and is also perfect as a snack-in-a-glass at any time. Papaya is a great source of beta-carotene and vitamin C.

1 small ripe papaya
250ml/8fl oz/1 cup cold almond milk yogurt
5ml/1 tsp honey or sugar

Serves 4

NUTRITIONAL INFORMATION:
Energy 92kcal/389kJ; Protein 1.4g; Carbohydrate 19.6g, of which sugars 6.9g; Fat 1.2g, of which saturates 0g; Cholesterol 0mg; Calcium 37mg; Fibre 3.7g; Sodium 37mg.

1 Cut the papaya in half lengthways, and remove the seeds and the white pith with a teaspoon.

2 Chop the papaya flesh roughly into small pieces, reserve a few pieces for a garnish and place the rest in a blender or large bowl.

3 Add the almond milk yogurt, 250ml/8fl oz/1 cup cold water and the honey or sugar and process in the blender, or with a stick blender, until smooth. Top with the papaya chunks and serve.

SOUPS

CHILLED ALMOND MILK AND GARLIC SOUP

This milky-white Moroccan soup is traditionally made from unstrained almond milk and is heavily laced with garlic. It is deliciously refreshing in hot weather.

3–4 slices day-old white bread,
   crusts removed
4 garlic cloves, peeled
60ml/4 tbsp olive oil
1 litre/1½ pints/4 cups unstrained
   almond milk
30ml/2 tbsp white wine vinegar
salt, to taste
small bunch sweet green grapes,
   halved and seeded and a
   handful raw unsalted blanched
   almonds, to garnish

Serves 4

1 Put the bread, garlic, olive oil and 150ml/¼ pint/⅔ cup of the almond milk in a large food processor or blender and blend to form a very smooth paste. Scrape down the sides.

2 With the motor running, add the rest of the almond milk until the mixture is smooth and has the consistency of single (light) cream. Add vinegar and salt to taste.

3 Chill, then serve garnished with grapes and almonds.

NUTRITIONAL INFORMATION: Energy 190kcal/790kJ; Protein 3g; Carbohydrate 15.3g, of which sugars 5.8g; Fat 13.5g, of which saturates 1.7g; Cholesterol 0mg; Calcium 22mg; Fibre 0.7g; Sodium 264mg.

CURRIED CAULIFLOWER AND CASHEW NUT MILK SOUP

This lightly spiced soup is both simple and satisfying. Serve with warm, crusty bread or with naan breads and garnish with sprigs of fresh coriander.

750ml/1¼ pints/3 cups cashew
   nut milk
1 large cauliflower, broken or cut
   into florets
15ml/1 tbsp garam masala
salt and ground black pepper,
   to taste
fresh coriander (cilantro) leaves,
   to garnish (optional)

Serves 4

1 Put the milk, cauliflower garam masala and seasoning in a pan and place over a medium heat. Bring to the boil, then reduce the heat, partially cover the pan and simmer for 20 minutes, until the cauliflower is tender.

2 Leave to cool for a few minutes, then process until smooth. Heat through without boiling. Garnish with fresh coriander.

NUTRITIONAL INFORMATION: Energy 197kcal/823kJ; Protein 10.1g; Carbohydrate 17.6g, of which sugars 10.1g; Fat 10.5g, of which saturates 2g; Cholesterol 0mg; Calcium 68mg; Fibre 5.2g; Sodium 175mg.

LEEK, OATMEAL AND OAT MILK BROTH

This broth is traditionally served with soda bread, but you could serve it with brown scones with oat milk (see page 118). Oat milk enhances the flavour of the broth.

600ml/1 pint/2½ cups oat milk
600ml/1 pint/2½ cups vegetable
   stock
30ml/2 tbsp medium pinhead
   oatmeal
6 large leeks, sliced into 2cm/¾in
   pieces
25g/1oz/2 tbsp sunflower
   margarine
salt and ground black pepper,
   to taste
pinch of ground mace
30ml/2 tbsp chopped fresh parsley
almond milk yogurt, to serve
   (optional)

Serves 4–6

1 Bring the oat milk and stock to the boil over a medium heat and sprinkle in the oatmeal. Stir well to prevent lumps forming, then simmer gently.

2 Wash the leeks in a bowl. Melt the sunflower margarine in a separate pan and cook the leeks over a gentle heat until they have softened slightly, then add them to the stock mixture. Simmer the mixture for 15–20 minutes, until the oatmeal is cooked. Extra stock can be added if the soup is too thick.

3 Season with salt, pepper and mace, stir in the chopped parsley and serve in warmed bowls. Decorate with a swirl of almond milk yogurt, if you like.

NUTRITIONAL INFORMATION: Energy 148kcal/618kJ; Protein 3.8g; Carbohydrate 9.9g, of which sugars 8.8g; Fat 6.1g, of which saturates 0.9g; Cholesterol 0mg; Calcium 55mg; Fibre 5.9g; Sodium 119mg.

PARSNIP SOUP WITH HAZELNUT BUTTER AND MILK

This lightly spiced creamy soup is perfect for a winter's day. It is thickened with a spoonful of hazelnut butter and finished with a scattering of crunchy croûtons. These can be made by frying cubes of day-old bread in very hot coconut oil.

900g/2lb parsnips
30ml/2 tbsp sunflower or
    coconut oil
1 onion, chopped
2 garlic cloves, crushed
10ml/2 tsp ground cumin
5ml/1 tsp ground coriander
15ml/1 tbsp smooth hazelnut
    butter
1.2 litres/2 pints/5 cups hot
    vegetable stock
about 150ml/¼ pint/⅔ cup hazelnut
    milk
salt and ground black pepper,
    to taste
chopped fresh chives or parsley
    and croûtons, to garnish

Serves 6

NUTRITIONAL INFORMATION:
Energy 170kcal/712kJ; Protein 3.6g;
Carbohydrate 23g, of which sugars
11.2g; Fat 7.5g, of which saturates
0.8g; Cholesterol 0mg; Calcium
70mg; Fibre 9.8g; Sodium 16mg.

1 Peel and thinly slice the parsnips. Heat the oil in a large, heavy pan and add the peeled parsnips and chopped onion with the crushed garlic. Cook over a gentle heat until the vegetables are softened but not coloured, stirring occasionally.

2 Add the ground cumin and coriander to the pan and cook, stirring for 1–2 minutes. Add the hazelnut butter, then gradually blend in the hot vegetable stock.

3 Cover and simmer for 20 minutes, or until the parsnip is soft. Remove from the heat and leave to cool slightly.

4 Purée the soup in a blender or food processor. Pour back into the rinsed-out pan and stir in the hazelnut milk. Check the consistency and add more hazelnut milk if it is too thick. Season to taste and reheat until steaming hot, but do not boil.

5 Ladle into warm soup bowls and serve immediately, garnished with chopped chives or parsley and croûtons.

FRESH MUSHROOM SOUP WITH HEMP SEED MILK

The earthy flavour of brown cap mushrooms is subtly enhanced with hemp seed milk and given a hint of aniseed with tarragon. Serve in small bowls with rolls as an appetizer or in larger portions with crusty bread for lunch.

4 shallots
15ml/1 tbsp sunflower or
    coconut oil
450g/1lb/6 cups brown cap
    (cremini) mushrooms,
    finely chopped
300ml/½ pint/1¼ cups vegetable
    stock
300ml/½ pint/1¼ cups hemp seed
    milk
15–30ml/1–2 tbsp chopped
    fresh tarragon, plus sprigs,
    to garnish
salt and ground black pepper,
    to taste

Serves 4

Cook's tip
Brown cap (cremini) mushrooms have a more robust flavour than cultivated ones, such as button (white), cap and flat mushrooms. Field (portobello) mushrooms are similar in appearance to cultivated flat mushrooms, but they are simply large brown cap mushrooms.

NUTRITIONAL INFORMATION:
Energy 138kcal/577kJ; Protein 6.5g; Carbohydrate 8.9g, of which sugars 7g; Fat 8.8g, of which saturates 1.2g; Cholesterol 0mg; Calcium 34.5mg; Fibre 3.6g; Sodium 133mg.

1 Finely chop the shallots. Heat the oil in a large pan, add the shallots and cook for 5 minutes, stirring occasionally.

2 Add the mushrooms and cook gently for 3 minutes, stirring, then add the stock and milk. Bring to the boil, then cover and simmer for about 20 minutes, until the vegetables are soft.

3 Stir in the chopped fresh tarragon and season to taste with salt and ground black pepper.

4 Allow the soup to cool slightly, then purée it in a blender or food processor, in batches if necessary, until smooth. Return to the rinsed-out pan and reheat gently, until steaming hot.

5 Ladle the soup into warmed bowls and serve immediately, garnished with sprigs of fresh tarragon.

ONION SOUP WITH ALMOND BUTTER AND MILK

This velvety-smooth soup proves that you don't need dairy to create a creamy dish. Almond butter gives it a wonderful silkiness that is complemented by the croûtes.

75g/3oz/6 tbsp sunflower margarine
1kg/2¼lb onions, sliced
1 fresh bay leaf
75ml/5 tbsp white vermouth
15ml/1 tbsp smooth almond butter
1 litre/1¾ pints/4 cups chicken or
    vegetable stock
salt and ground black pepper,
    to taste
150ml/¼ pint/⅔ cup almond milk
chopped fresh chives, to garnish
croûtes (see Cook's tip), to serve

Serves 4

Cook's tip
To make the croûtes, preheat the oven to 200°C/400°F/ Gas 6. Thinly slice some French bread at an angle, brush with olive oil and bake for 12–15 minutes. For garlic croûtes, mix 1–2 crushed garlic cloves with sunflower margarine and thinly spread this over the bread instead of the oil.

NUTRITIONAL INFORMATION:
Energy 277kcal/1147kJ; Protein 4g; Carbohydrate 21.2g, of which sugars 14.6g; Fat 18.4g, of which saturates 3.5g; Cholesterol 0mg; Calcium 65mg; Fibre 5.4g; Sodium 137mg.

1 Melt the sunflower margarine in a large pan. Add the onions and bay leaf and stir to coat. Cover the pan and cook very gently for 30 minutes, stirring occasionally, until the onions are soft and tender but not browned. Remove slightly less than a quarter of the onions and set aside.

2 Pour the vermouth into the pan, increase the heat and boil until the liquid has almost evaporated. Add the almond butter.

3 Pour in a little of the stock. Stir until the almond butter is mixed in, then pour in the rest of the stock and season to taste. Bring to the boil, lower the heat, cover and simmer for 5 minutes.

4 Leave to cool a little, then discard the bay leaf and blend the soup, until it is very smooth. Return the soup to the rinsed pan.

5 Cook the reserved onions in a non-stick frying pan, until just starting to turn golden. Add to the soup with the almond milk and reheat gently until hot. Taste and adjust the seasoning.

6 Ladle the soup into warmed soup bowls and garnish with chopped fresh chives. Serve with croûtes.

CARROT, APPLE AND CASHEW NUT MILK SOUP

A combination of sweet carrots and tart apples make this as healthy as it is tasty. It can be prepared in advance, then reheated with the cashew nut milk just before serving.

15ml/1 tbsp sunflower or
    coconut oil
1 onion, roughly chopped
1 garlic clove, roughly chopped
500g/1¼lb carrots, chopped
2 small, slightly tart eating
    apples, peeled, cored and
    roughly chopped
750ml/1¼ pints/3 cups vegetable
    stock
100ml/3½fl oz/scant ½ cup
    unsweetened apple juice
salt and ground white pepper,
    to taste
150ml/¼ pint/⅔ cup cashew nut milk
15ml/1 tbsp pumpkin seeds and
    15ml/1 tbsp chopped fresh
    chives, to garnish

Serves 4

NUTRITIONAL INFORMATION:
Energy 148kcal/618kJ; Protein 2.6g;
Carbohydrate 24.6g, of which
sugars 21.1g; Fat 5.1g, of which
saturates 0.8g; Cholesterol 0mg;
Calcium 49mg; Fibre 6.2g; Sodium
192mg.

1 Heat the oil in a pan over a medium heat. Add the onion and cook for 5 minutes, until softened. Add the garlic and cook for a few minutes more. Stir in the carrot and apple.

2 Add the stock and apple juice, then season with salt and ground white pepper. Bring to the boil, reduce the heat and simmer for 15 minutes.

3 Add the cashew nut milk and heat the soup until it just begins to boil again. Blend the soup with a hand blender. If it seems too thick, add some more stock or cashew nut milk.

4 Heat a frying pan over a medium heat and dry-fry the pumpkin seeds for 3 minutes, until toasted, stirring occasionally.

5 Ladle the soup into warmed bowls and garnish it with the toasted pumpkin seeds and some chopped fresh chives. Serve the soup immediately.

SEAFOOD CHOWDER WITH COCONUT MILK

Delicate seafood is complemented by vegetables and creamy coconut milk in this flavour-packed soup. Choose firm white fish, which will keep its shape during cooking.

30ml/2 tbsp coconut or
   sunflower oil
1 large onion, chopped
115g/4oz bacon, rind removed,
   diced
4 celery sticks, diced
2 large potatoes, diced
450g/1lb ripe, juicy tomatoes,
   chopped or 400g/14oz can
   chopped tomatoes
450ml/¾ pint/2 cups fish stock
225g/8oz shellfish, such as mussels,
   prawns (shrimp) or scallops
300ml/½ pint/1¼ cups coconut milk
15ml/1 tbsp cornflour (cornstarch)
450g/1lb white fish fillets, such
   as cod, plaice, flounder or
   haddock, skinned and cut into
   small chunks
salt and ground black pepper,
   to taste
coconut cream and chopped
   parsley, to garnish

Serves 4–6

1 Heat the oil in a large pan, add the onion, bacon, celery and potato and coat with the oil. Cover and leave to sweat over a gentle heat for 5–10 minutes, without colouring.

2 Purée the tomatoes in a blender, and strain them to remove the skin and pips. Add the puréed tomato and stock to the pan. Bring to the boil, cover and leave to simmer gently until the potatoes are tender, skimming the top occasionally as required.

3 To prepare the mussels, scrub the shells under running water and discard any that do not open when tapped. Prepare the prawns by plunging them briefly in a pan of boiling water. Cool and peel. The scallops can be left whole.

4 Put the mussels into a shallow, heavy pan, without adding any liquid. Cover and cook over a high heat for a few minutes, shaking occasionally, until all the mussels have opened. Discard any that fail to open. Remove the mussels from their shells. Add all the prepared shellfish to the soup.

5 Blend together the coconut milk and cornflour, stir into the soup and bring to the boil. Reduce the heat, add the fish, cover and simmer for a few minutes or until the fish is tender. Season to taste. Serve garnished with coconut cream and some parsley.

NUTRITIONAL INFORMATION:
Energy 215kcal/899kJ; Protein 3.9g;
Carbohydrate 21.3g, of which
sugars 10.6g; Fat 13.3g, of which
saturates 7.7g; Cholesterol 32mg;
Calcium 92mg; Fibre 7.3g; Sodium
74mg.

PUMPKIN, CHICKEN AND PUMPKIN SEED MILK SOUP

Ideal for a mid-week supper or weekend lunch, this comforting soup is a complete meal in itself, served with warm bread rolls.

30ml/2 tbsp sunflower oil
6 green cardamom pods
2 leeks, chopped
350g/12oz seeded and skinned pumpkin, cubed
750ml/1¼ pints/3 cups chicken stock
115g/4oz/generous ½ cup basmati rice, soaked
salt and ground black pepper, to taste
350ml/12fl oz/1½ cups pumpkin seed milk
200g/7oz cooked chicken, roughly chopped
strips of pared orange rind and cracked black pepper, to garnish
wholemeal (whole-wheat) or granary warm bread rolls, to serve

Serves 4

Cook's tip
Once made, chicken stock will keep in an airtight container in the refrigerator for 3–4 days. Alternatively, use stock (bouillon) cubes.

NUTRITIONAL INFORMATION:
Energy 308kcal/1289kJ; Protein 18.8g; Carbohydrate 29.9g, of which sugars 3.8g; Fat 12.9g, of which saturates 1.5g; Cholesterol 35mg; Calcium 57mg; Fibre 5g; Sodium 443mg.

1 Heat the oil in a pan and fry the cardamom pods for 3 minutes, until slightly swollen. Add the leeks and pumpkin.

2 Cook, stirring, for 3–4 minutes over a medium heat, then lower the heat, cover and sweat for 5 minutes, until the pumpkin is soft.

3 Pour 600ml/1 pint/2½ cups of the stock into the pan. Bring to the boil, then lower the heat, cover the pan and simmer gently for 10–15 minutes, until the pumpkin is soft.

4 Pour the remaining stock into a measuring jug (cup) and make up with water to 300ml/½ pint/1¼ cups. Drain the rice and put it into a pan. Pour in the stock, bring to the boil, then simmer for about 10 minutes until the rice is tender. Add seasoning to taste.

5 Remove the cardamom pods and process the soup until smooth. Pour the soup back into a clean pan and stir in the pumpkin seed milk, chicken and rice (with any stock). Heat until simmering.

6 Ladle into warmed bowls, garnish with orange rind and cracked black pepper, and serve with warm bread rolls.

SNACKS AND SALADS

AUBERGINE DIP WITH TAHINI AND ALMOND YOGURT

This smoky aubergine and tahini dip is also known as baba ganoush. Some cooks add chopped flat leaf parsley and others sharpen it with lemon juice, or make it creamy with thick yogurt. This one contains all of these for maximum flavour.

2 large aubergines (eggplants)
30–45ml/2–3 tbsp tahini
juice of 1–2 lemons
45ml/3 tbsp thick almond milk
    yogurt (see Cook's tip)
2 cloves garlic, crushed
1 bunch flat leaf parsley, chopped
salt and ground black pepper,
    to taste
olive oil, for drizzling

Serves 4

Cook's tip
To make thick almond milk yogurt, line a plastic sieve (strainer) with a piece of muslin (cheesecloth) and place it over a bowl. Spoon in 90ml/6 tbsp almond milk yogurt (see page 37). Leave the bowl in the refrigerator for 1–2 hours to drain; you should then be left with about 45ml/3 tbsp thick almond milk yogurt in the muslin. Discard the liquid in the bowl.

1 Place the aubergines on a hot griddle, or directly over a gas flame or charcoal grill, turning them from time to time, until they are soft to the touch and the skin is charred and flaky.

2 Place the charred aubergines in a plastic bag and leave for a few minutes to sweat. When they are cool enough to handle, hold them by the stems under cold running water and peel off and discard the skin. Squeeze out the excess water, then chop the flesh to a pulp.

3 In a bowl, beat the tahini with the lemon juice – the mixture stiffens at first, then loosens to a creamy paste. Beat in the thick almond milk yogurt and then, using a fork, beat in the aubergine pulp until everything is well combined.

4 Add the garlic and parsley (reserving a little to garnish), season with salt and pepper and beat the mixture thoroughly.

5 Transfer the dip to a serving dish, drizzle a little olive oil over the top to keep it moist and sprinkle with the reserved parsley.

NUTRITIONAL INFORMATION:
Energy 202kcal/840kJ; Protein 6.6g; Carbohydrate 5.3g, of which sugars 3.4g; Fat 17.5g, of which saturates 2.5g; Cholesterol 0mg; Calcium 206mg; Fibre 6.5g; Sodium 12mg.

SPICY WALNUT YOGURT DIP

Roasted peppers and walnuts combine to make this wonderfully spiced dip, 'muhammara', an Arab favourite since medieval times. It includes pomegranate molasses, a fragrant, slightly sour and tangy syrup.

2 red (bell) peppers
1 red chilli, seeded and very
   finely chopped
2 cloves garlic, crushed with salt
125g/4½oz raw unsalted walnuts,
   roughly chopped
30ml/2 tbsp toasted breadcrumbs
15ml/1 tbsp pomegranate molasses
juice of ½ a lemon
5ml/1 tsp sugar
45ml/3 tbsp olive oil, plus extra
   for drizzling
pinch of salt
250ml/8fl oz/1 cup thick walnut
   milk yogurt (see Cook's tip)
sticks of carrot, celery and (bell)
   pepper and spring onions
   (scallions), to serve

Serves 6

Cook's tip
Prepare the thick walnut yogurt using the method for nut milk yogurt on page 37, starting with 475ml/16fl oz/ 2 cups walnut milk. The yogurt should be thick, but not too thick, so check after 1 hour. Use as much or as little as you like in the dip.

NUTRITIONAL INFORMATION:
Energy 291kcal/1210kJ; Protein 4.9g; Carbohydrate 22.2g, of which sugars 11.9g; Fat 20.9g, of which saturates 2.4g; Cholesterol 0mg; Calcium 36mg; Fibre 3.4g; Sodium 86mg.

1 Place the peppers directly over a gas flame and roast them until the skin is charred and buckled. Put the peppers in a plastic bag and leave them to sweat for 5 minutes, to loosen the skins. Peel off the skins and remove the stalks and seeds. Chop the pepper flesh into very small pieces.

2 Using a mortar and pestle, pound the chopped peppers with the chilli, garlic and walnuts to a fairly smooth paste. You could use a food processor for this, but pulse rather than blend for a rough, chopped consistency.

3 Beat the breadcrumbs, pomegranate molasses, lemon juice and sugar into the pepper and walnut paste. Drizzle the oil into the mixture, beating all the time, until it is thick and creamy.

4 Add the thick walnut milk yogurt and stir to combine. Check the seasoning, drizzle a little olive oil over the top and serve with sticks of carrot, celery and pepper and spring onions.

TAHINI HUMMUS

This easy-to-prepare hummus is rich in protein, vitamins and minerals, so makes a super-healthy snack or lunch – ideal if you are vegetarian. Serve with crudités, such as celery, carrot and cucumber sticks, olives and some toasted pieces of pitta bread.

225g/8oz can chickpeas
2 garlic cloves, coarsely crushed
90ml/6 tbsp lemon juice
60ml/4 tbsp tahini, for recipe see
    page 49
75ml/5 tbsp olive oil, plus extra
    to serve
5ml/1 tsp ground cumin
salt and ground black pepper,
    to taste
paprika, to garnish
crudités, lightly toasted pitta bread
    and olives, to serve

Serves 4

Variation
For a nuttier flavour, substitute smooth peanut butter for the tahini paste.

NUTRITIONAL INFORMATION:
Energy 364kcal/1510kJ; Protein 10g; Carbohydrate 15g, of which sugars 3g; Fat 29g, of which saturates 4g; Cholesterol 0mg; Calcium 141mg; Fibre 2g; Sodium 8mg.

1 Drain the chickpeas, reserving the liquid from the can, and put them into a blender or food processor. Blend to a smooth paste, adding a small amount of the reserved liquid, if necessary.

2 Add the garlic and lemon juice to the blender or food processor and process until fairly smooth. Stop and scrape down the sides of the machine, then add the tahini and blend again.

3 With the machine running, gradually add 45ml/3 tbsp of the olive oil through the feeder tube or lid. Add the cumin and season with salt and ground black pepper. Process to mix.

4 Spoon and scrape the hummus into a serving bowl. Cover with clear film (plastic wrap) and chill until required.

5 When you are ready to serve, drizzle the hummus with olive oil and garnish with paprika, then serve it with crudités, lightly toasted pitta bread and olives.

SEAFOOD AND CASHEW NUT MILK PURÉE

This unusual dip is based on a Brazilian classic called 'vatapá' and can be eaten as an appetizer or main course. It can also be diluted with more fish stock and coconut milk and served as a thick soup, accompanied by crusty bread.

600ml/1 pint/2½ cups fish stock
450g/1lb white fish fillets
65g/2½oz dried shrimp
75g/3oz/¾ cup roasted, skinned
    unsalted peanuts
75g/3oz/¾ cup roasted unsalted
    cashew nuts
½ loaf day-old French bread, torn
    into pieces and soaked in
    475ml/16fl oz/2 cups cashew
    nut milk
2.5ml/½ tsp fresh root ginger, grated
1.5ml/¼ tsp freshly grated nutmeg
30ml/2 tbsp lime juice
15ml/1 tbsp coconut oil
150ml/¼ pint/⅔ cup coconut milk
5ml/1 tsp hot pepper sauce
salt and ground black pepper
large cooked prawns (shrimp) and
    lime wedges, to garnish

Serves 8

Variation
For a slightly less expensive dish, use peanut milk instead of cashew nut milk.

NUTRITIONAL INFORMATION:
Energy 422kcal/1780kJ; Protein 27.3g; Carbohydrate 48.6g, of which sugars 5.9g; Fat 14.7g, of which saturates 3.7g; Cholesterol 67mg; Calcium 210mg; Fibre 2.7g; Sodium 918mg.

1 Heat the stock in a medium pan, add the fish and poach it for 3–5 minutes, until just cooked.

2 Remove the fish to a plate with a slotted spoon. Reserve the stock. When the fish is cool enough to handle, flake and set aside.

3 Put the dried shrimp, peanuts and cashew nuts in a food processor and blend until finely ground. Squeeze the excess milk out of the bread and reserve it. Add the bread to the food processor with the fish. Blend to a smooth purée.

4 Scrape the purée into a pan and gradually add enough of the reserved cashew nut milk to achieve a thick, creamy consistency. If necessary, add some of the reserved fish stock as well.

5 Stir in the grated ginger and nutmeg, lime juice and coconut oil and cook for another 2 minutes. Add the coconut milk and hot pepper sauce and cook for a further 4 minutes. Spoon into a bowl and garnish with cooked prawns and lime wedges.

HADDOCK AND SALMON TERRINE WITH CASHEW CREAM

A stunning centrepiece for a summer buffet, this is delicious served with dill-flavoured cashew cream. Full-bodied cashew nut milk is used to keep the fish moist.

15ml/1 tbsp sunflower oil,
   for greasing
350g/12oz oak-smoked salmon
900g/2lb haddock fillets, skinned
salt and ground white pepper,
   to taste
2 eggs, lightly beaten
90ml/6 tbsp full-bodied cashew
   nut milk
30ml/2 tbsp drained capers
30ml/2 tbsp drained soft green or
   pink peppercorns
dill-flavoured cashew cream
   (see Cook's tip), to serve
peppercorns and fresh dill and
   rocket (arugula), to garnish

Serves 10–12

Cook's tip
For dill-flavoured cashew
cream follow the recipe for
cashew nut cream on page
51, then stir in 45ml/3 tbsp
chopped fresh dill.

1 Preheat the oven to 200°C/400°F/Gas 6. Grease a 1 litre/1¾ pint/4 cup loaf tin (pan) or terrine with the oil. Use some of the salmon to line the tin or terrine; let some of the ends overhang the mould. Reserve the remaining smoked salmon.

2 Cut two long slices of haddock the length of the tin or terrine and set aside. Cut the rest of the haddock into small pieces. Season all the haddock with salt and pepper.

3 Combine the eggs, full-bodied cashew nut milk, capers and green or pink peppercorns in a bowl. Season, then stir in the small pieces of haddock. Spoon the mixture into the mould until it is one-third full. Smooth the surface with a spatula.

4 Wrap the long haddock fillets in the reserved smoked salmon. Lay them on top of the layer of fish mixture. Fill the tin or terrine with the rest of the fish mixture, smooth the surface and fold the overhanging pieces of smoked salmon over the top. Cover tightly with a double thickness of foil. Tap the tin or terrine to settle the contents.

5 Stand the tin or terrine in a roasting pan and pour in boiling water to come halfway up the sides. Place in the oven and cook for 45 minutes–1 hour, until the filling is just set.

6 Take the tin or terrine out of the roasting pan, but do not remove the foil cover. Place two or three large, heavy cans on top of the foil to weight it and leave until cold. Chill in the refrigerator for 24 hours.

7 About an hour before serving, remove the tin or terrine from the refrigerator, lift off the weights and remove the foil. Carefully invert the tin or terrine on to a serving plate and lift off the mould. Cut the terrine into thick slices using a sharp knife and serve, garnished with dill-flavoured cashew cream, peppercorns and fronds of dill and rocket leaves.

NUTRITIONAL INFORMATION: Energy 173kcal/729kJ; Protein 24.3g; Carbohydrate 4.1g, of which sugars 2.2g; Fat 7.2g, of which saturates 1.4g; Cholesterol 76mg; Calcium 33mg; Fibre 0.3g; Sodium 676mg.

PEANUT BUTTER AND TOFU CUTLETS

These delicious protein-packed patties make a satisfying vegetarian mid-week meal served with lightly steamed green vegetables or a colourful mixed salad.

90g/3½oz/½ cup brown rice
15ml/1 tbsp vegetable oil
1 onion, finely chopped
1 garlic clove, crushed
115g/4oz/¾ cup raw unsalted
   skinned peanuts
115g/4oz/½ cup crunchy peanut
   butter
250g/9oz firm silken tofu
30ml/2 tbsp soy sauce
small bunch of fresh coriander
   (cilantro) or parsley,
   chopped (optional)
30ml/2 tbsp olive oil, for
   shallow-frying
tomato and red onion salad or
   steamed green vegetables,
   to serve

Serves 4

NUTRITIONAL INFORMATION:
Energy 754kcal/3142kJ; Protein
45.1g; Carbohydrate 43.2g, of
which sugars 6.7g; Fat 47.6g, of
which saturates 6.5g; Cholesterol
0mg; Calcium 253mg; Fibre 3.8g;
Sodium 643mg.

1 Cook the rice according to the packet instructions until tender, then drain. Heat the vegetable oil in a large, heavy frying pan and cook the onion and garlic over a low heat, stirring occasionally, for about 5 minutes, until softened and golden.

2 Meanwhile, spread out the peanuts on a baking sheet and toast under the grill (broiler) for a few minutes, until browned. Place the peanuts, peanut butter, onion, garlic, rice, tofu, soy sauce and fresh coriander or parsley, if using, in a blender or food processor and process until a thick paste forms.

3 Divide the paste into eight equal-size mounds and form each mound into a cutlet shape or square.

4 Heat the olive oil for shallow-frying in a large, heavy frying pan. Add the cutlets, in two batches if necessary, and cook for 5–10 minutes on each side, until golden and heated through.

5 Remove from the pan and drain on kitchen paper. Keep warm while you cook the remaining batch, then serve immediately with a tomato and red onion salad or steamed green vegetables.

CHICKEN SATAY

Marinated, skewered and grilled chicken served with a peanut sauce is popular throughout South-east Asia. Everything can be made a day in advance.

350g/12oz chicken breast fillet,
   cut into pieces 4 x 2.5 x 1cm/
   1½ x 1 x ½in
12–16 bamboo or wooden
   skewers, soaked in water
flat leaf parsley, to garnish

FOR THE MARINADE
10ml/2 tsp ground coriander
10ml/2 tsp ground cumin
2.5ml/½ tsp ground turmeric
2.5ml/½ tsp chilli powder
120ml/4fl oz/½ cup coconut milk
2.5ml/½ tsp salt
5ml/1 tsp sugar
30ml/2 tbsp sunflower oil

FOR THE SAUCE
50g/2oz creamed coconut,
   roughly chopped
5ml/1 tsp soft dark brown sugar
90ml/6 tbsp crunchy peanut butter
30ml/2 tbsp soy sauce
1.5ml/¼ tsp dried chilli flakes
1 garlic clove, crushed
5ml/1 tsp finely chopped fresh
   lemon grass or finely grated
   lemon rind

Makes 12–16 sticks

NUTRITIONAL INFORMATION:
Energy 80kcal/334kJ; Protein 6.8g;
Carbohydrate 1.4g, of which sugars
1g; Fat 5.3g, of which saturates
2.6g; Cholesterol 15mg; Calcium
4mg; Fibre 0g; Sodium 167mg.

1 Thoroughly blend together all the ingredients for the marinade in a non-metallic dish. Add the chicken, cover and leave to marinate in the refrigerator for several hours or overnight.

2 To make the sauce, put the creamed coconut in a heatproof serving bowl and pour over 300ml/½ pint/1¼ cups boiling water. Stir until dissolved. Add the sugar and stir again.

3 Add the peanut butter, soy sauce, chilli flakes, garlic and lemon grass or lemon rind and stir to combine. Leave to cool and thicken at room temperature.

4 Thread three or four pieces of chicken on to each stick, pressing them together. Grill over hot coals or under a hot grill (broiler) for 8 minutes, turning once.

5 Arrange the hot satay sticks on a plate and garnish with flat leaf parsley. Serve with the peanut sauce.

GADO-GADO

This vegetable salad is of Indonesian origin, but it is also very popular in Malaysia and Singapore. It is distinguished by the crunchy peanut butter and coconut sauce.

½ cucumber
2 pears or 175g/6oz yam bean
1–2 eating apples
juice of ½ lemon
mixed salad leaves
6 small tomatoes, cut into wedges
3 slices fresh pineapple, cored and
   cut into wedges
3 eggs, hard-boiled and shelled
175g/6oz egg noodles, cooked,
   cooled and chopped
deep-fried onions

FOR THE PEANUT SAUCE
2 fresh chillies, seeded and chopped,
   or 15ml/1 tbsp chilli sambal
300ml/½ pint/1¼ cups coconut milk
350g/12oz/1¼ cups crunchy
   peanut butter
15ml/1 tbsp dark soy sauce
10ml/2 tsp dark muscovado
   (molasses) sugar
5ml/1 tsp tamarind pulp, soaked in
   45ml/3 tbsp warm water
30ml/2 tbsp crushed raw unsalted
   skinned peanuts

Serves 6

1 To make the peanut sauce, put the finely chopped chillies or chilli sambal in a small pan. Pour in the coconut milk, then stir in the peanut butter. Heat the mixture very gently, stirring, until well blended.

2 Continue heating the sauce until it just starts to simmer, stirring frequently. Stir in the soy sauce and dark muscovado sugar. Strain in the tamarind liquid, discarding any pulp left in the sieve (strainer), and mix well.

3 Turn off the heat and spoon the sauce into a serving bowl. Sprinkle the crushed peanuts over the top.

4 To make the salad, remove the core from the cucumber and peel the pears or yam bean. Cut them into matchsticks. Core and then finely shred the apple and sprinkle with the lemon juice to prevent the shreds from discolouring.

5 Spread a bed of salad leaves on a flat platter or a section of banana leaf, then pile the fruit and vegetables on top. Add the sliced or quartered eggs, the noodles and the deep-fried onions.

6 Serve immediately, with the peanut sauce to spoon over each portion.

NUTRITIONAL INFORMATION: Energy 240kcal/1003kJ; Protein 13.5g; Carbohydrate 17.3g, of which sugars 12.5g; Fat 13.1g, of which saturates 3.4g; Cholesterol 166mg; Calcium 73mg; Fibre 5.9g; Sodium 611mg.

Variation: Refreshing Fruit Salad with Peanut Sauce
Finely slice 1 green mango, 1 firm, ripe papaya and 2 star fruits (carambolas). Skin and core ½ pineapple and cut it into chunks, then segment ½ pomelo. Peel, seed and slice 1 small cucumber and finely slice 1 yam bean. Toss all the ingredients with a handful of beansprouts and the peanut sauce given above. Serves 6.

NUTRITIONAL INFORMATION: Energy 321kcal/1354kJ; Protein 12.3g; Carbohydrate 30g, of which sugars 27.2g; Fat 17.7g, of which saturates 3.3g; Cholesterol 8mg; Calcium 91mg; Fibre 6.2g; Sodium 81mg.

SPROUT SALAD WITH CASHEW NUT CREAM DRESSING

Sprouting pulses and grains increases their nutritional content drastically and they become great sources of vitamins C and B. Here they are served with a high-protein cashew nut dressing, transforming this simple salad into an extra-healthy meal.

115g/4oz/¾ cup raw unsalted
    cashew nuts
½ cucumber
1 red (bell) pepper, seeded and
    diced
90g/3½oz mung bean, aduki bean
    or chickpea sprouts
juice of ½ lemon
small bunch fresh parsley,
    coriander (cilantro) or basil,
    finely chopped
5ml/1 tsp sesame, sunflower or
    pumpkin seeds

Serves 1–2

Cook's tips
• There are all kinds of sprouts, and beansprouts are one of the most readily available commercially. Rinse in cold water before using in salads and other recipes.
• Choose fresh, crisp sprouts with the bean or seed still attached. Avoid any that are slightly slimy or smell musty. They will keep for up to 2 days in a plastic bag in the refrigerator.

NUTRITIONAL INFORMATION:
Energy 402Kcal/1668kJ; Protein 14.7g; Carbohydrate 18.9g, of which sugars 10.1g; Fat 30.2g, of which saturates 6g; Cholesterol 0mg; Calcium 86mg; Fibre 5.2g; Sodium 181mg.

1 Put the cashew nuts in a heatproof bowl, pour over 100ml/3½fl oz/scant ½ cup boiling water, then cover with clear film (plastic wrap) and leave them to soak for a few hours, preferably overnight, in a refrigerator, until softened.

2 Process the nuts with the soaking water in a food processor or blender to form a smooth sauce. Add a little more water if necessary; it should be quite thick.

3 Peel away the cucumber skin in strips lengthways to produce a striped effect. Cut the cucumber into dice.

4 Place the diced pepper, sprouts, cucumber and lemon juice in a bowl and toss together.

5 Serve immediately with the cashew cream dressing and scatter with the fresh herbs and seeds.

CHICKEN SALAD WITH NUTS AND COCONUT CREAM

The sauce in this Thai-style salad is made from coconut cream, sharpened with lime juice and with the distinctive taste of fish sauce. The chicken is marinated to tenderize and add flavour to the dish. Assemble just before serving so that the lettuce stays crisp.

4 skinless, boneless chicken
   breast portions
2 garlic cloves, crushed
30ml/2 tbsp soy sauce
30ml/2 tbsp vegetable oil
120ml/4fl oz/½ cup coconut cream
30ml/2 tbsp Thai fish sauce
juice of 1 lime
30ml/2 tbsp light muscovado
   (brown) sugar
115g/4oz/½ cup water chestnuts,
   sliced
50g/2oz/½ cup raw unsalted
   cashew nuts, roasted and
   coarsely chopped
4 shallots, thinly sliced
4 kaffir lime leaves, thinly sliced
1 lemon grass stalk, thinly sliced
5ml/1 tsp chopped fresh galangal
1 large fresh red chilli, seeded and
   finely chopped
2 spring onions (scallions),
   thinly sliced
10–12 fresh mint leaves, torn
1 lettuce, separated into leaves,
   to serve
2 fresh red chillies, seeded and
   sliced, to garnish (optional)

Serves 4–6

NUTRITIONAL INFORMATION:
Energy 349kcal/1453kJ; Protein
24.3g; Carbohydrate 11.5g, of
which sugars 9.8g; Fat 23.2g, of
which saturates 12.3g; Cholesterol
43mg; Calcium 49mg; Fibre 1.7g;
Sodium 200mg.

1 Place the chicken breast portions in a large dish. Rub them with the garlic, soy sauce and 15ml/1 tbsp of the oil. Cover with clear film (plastic wrap) and leave to marinate in the refrigerator for 1–2 hours.

2 Heat the remaining oil in a wok or frying pan and stir-fry the chicken for 3–4 minutes on each side, or until cooked. Remove and set aside to cool.

3 In a pan, heat the coconut cream, fish sauce, lime juice and sugar. Stir until the sugar has dissolved, then set aside.

4 Tear the chicken into strips and put them in a bowl. Add the water chestnuts, cashew nuts, shallots, kaffir lime leaves, lemon grass, galangal, red chilli, spring onions and mint leaves.

5 Pour the dressing over the mixture and toss well. Serve the chicken mixture on a bed of lettuce leaves and garnish with chillies, if using.

MAIN COURSES

PUMPKIN, PEANUT AND COCONUT MILK CURRY

Rich, sweet, spicy and fragrant, the flavours of this Thai-style curry will be relished by meat-eaters as well as vegetarians. Serve with basmati rice or noodles for supper.

30ml/2 tbsp groundnut (peanut) oil
4 garlic cloves, crushed
4 shallots, finely chopped
30ml/2 tbsp yellow curry paste
2 kaffir lime leaves, torn
15ml/1 tbsp chopped fresh
  galangal
450g/1lb pumpkin, peeled, seeded
  and diced
225g/8oz sweet potatoes, diced
400ml/14fl oz/1⅔ cups near-boiling
  vegetable stock
300ml/½ pint/1¼ cups coconut milk
90g/3½oz/1½ cups chestnut
  mushrooms, sliced
15ml/1 tbsp soy sauce
30ml/2 tbsp Thai fish sauce
90g/3½oz/scant 1 cup roasted
  unsalted peanuts, chopped
50g/2oz/⅓ cup pumpkin seeds,
  toasted, and fresh green or red
  chilli flowers, to garnish

Serves 4

Cook's tip
To make chilli flowers, hold
each by the stem and slit
the chilli in half lengthways,
keeping the stem end intact.
Continue slitting the chilli in
the same way to make strips.

NUTRITIONAL INFORMATION:
Energy 357kcal/1489kJ; Protein
12.1g; Carbohydrate 28g, of which
sugars 14g; Fat 22.6g, of which
saturates 3.8g; Cholesterol 0mg;
Calcium 103mg; Fibre 5.5g;
Sodium 1121mg.

1 Heat the oil in a large pan. Add the garlic and shallots and cook over a medium heat, stirring occasionally, for 10 minutes, until softened and beginning to turn golden.

2 Add the yellow curry paste to the pan and stir-fry over a medium heat for 30 seconds, until fragrant.

3 Add the lime leaves, galangal, pumpkin and sweet potato. Stir in the hot stock and 150ml/¼ pint/⅔ cup of the coconut milk. Bring to the boil, lower the heat and gently simmer for 15 minutes.

4 Stir in the chestnut mushrooms, soy sauce and Thai fish sauce, then add the peanuts and pour in the remaining coconut milk. Cover and cook for a further 15–20 minutes, or until all the vegetables are tender.

5 Spoon the curry into warmed serving bowls, garnish with the pumpkin seeds and chilli flowers, and serve immediately.

ROASTED VEGETABLES WITH PEANUT SAUCE

Roasting vegetables enhances their flavour and brings out their natural sweetness. The spicy peanut butter sauce provides a contrast in both taste and texture.

1 long, slender aubergine
   (eggplant), partially peeled and
   cut into long strips
2 courgettes (zucchini), partially
   peeled and cut into long strips
1 sweet potato, cut into long strips
2 leeks, trimmed and halved
   widthways and lengthways
2 garlic cloves, chopped
25g/1oz fresh root ginger, peeled
   and chopped
salt
60ml/4 tbsp vegetable or
   groundnut (peanut) oil
30ml/3 tbsp roasted unsalted
   peanuts, coarsely ground,
   to garnish
fresh crusty bread, to serve

FOR THE SAUCE
4 garlic cloves, chopped
2–3 red chillies, seeded and
   chopped
5ml/1 tsp shrimp paste
115g/4oz/½ cup crunchy peanut
   butter
salt and ground black pepper,
   to taste

Serves 4

....
NUTRITIONAL INFORMATION:
Energy 435kcal/1809kJ; Protein
14.9g; Carbohydrate 22.7g, of
which sugars 10.7g; Fat 32.3g, of
which saturates 6.2g; Cholesterol
6mg; Calcium 97mg; Fibre 7.8g;
Sodium 180mg.
....

1 Preheat the oven to 200°C/400°F/Gas 6. Arrange the prepared vegetables in a shallow oven dish.

2 Using a mortar and pestle or food processor, grind the garlic and ginger to a paste, then smear it evenly over the vegetables. Sprinkle with a little salt and pour over the oil.

3 Place the dish in the oven for about 45 minutes, until the vegetables are tender and slightly browned – toss them in the oil halfway through cooking.

4 Make the sauce. Using a mortar and pestle or food processor, grind the garlic and chillies to a paste then beat in the other ingredients, with salt and pepper to taste. Blend with water to pouring (half-and-half) cream consistency.

5 Arrange the vegetables on a serving dish and drizzle the sauce over them. Garnish with ground peanuts and serve warm with crusty bread.

MUSHROOM, COURGETTE AND ALMOND MILK LASAGNE

This healthy vegetarian dish is topped with almond milk sauce. It is ideal for a family meal or casual entertaining, as it can be made several hours in advance.

8 no pre-cook lasagne sheets
fresh oregano leaves, to garnish

FOR THE TOMATO SAUCE
15g/½oz dried porcini mushrooms
120ml/4fl oz/½ cup hot water
30ml/2 tbsp olive oil
1 onion, chopped
1 carrot, chopped
1 celery stick, chopped
2 x 400g/14oz cans chopped
  tomatoes
15ml/1 tbsp tomato purée (paste)
5ml/1 tsp dried basil

FOR THE VEGETABLE MIXTURE
45ml/3 tbsp olive oil
450g/1lb courgettes (zucchini),
  thinly sliced
salt and ground black pepper,
  to taste
1 onion, finely chopped
450g/1lb/6 cups chestnut
  mushrooms, thinly sliced
2 garlic cloves, crushed

FOR THE WHITE SAUCE
40g/1½oz/3 tbsp sunflower
  margarine
40g/1½oz/⅓ cup plain
  (all-purpose) flour
900ml/1½ pints/3¾ cups
  almond milk
salt and ground black pepper,
  to taste

Serves 6

1 To make the tomato sauce, put the dried porcini mushrooms in a bowl. Pour over the hot water and soak for 15 minutes. Tip the porcini and liquid into a sieve (strainer) set over a bowl and squeeze the mushrooms with your hands to release as much liquid as possible. Chop the mushrooms finely and set aside. Pour the soaking liquid through a fine sieve and reserve.

2 Heat the olive oil in a pan, add the chopped onion, carrot and celery and fry for about 10 minutes, until softened. Place in a food processor with the tomatoes, tomato purée, dried basil, porcini and soaking liquid, and blend to a purée.

3 For the vegetable mixture, heat 15ml/1 tbsp of the olive oil in a large pan. Add half the courgette slices and season to taste. Cook over a medium heat for 5–8 minutes, until lightly coloured on both sides. Remove to a bowl. Repeat this process with the remaining courgettes and 15ml/1 tbsp olive oil.

4 Heat the remaining 15ml/1 tbsp olive oil in the pan and cook the onion for 3 minutes, stirring. Add the chestnut mushrooms and garlic and cook for 5 minutes. Add to the courgettes.

5 For the white sauce, melt the margarine in a large pan, then add the flour and cook, stirring for 1 minute. Gradually whisk in the almond milk, then bring to the boil and cook, stirring, until the sauce is smooth and thick. Season to taste.

6 Preheat the oven to 190°C/375°F/Gas 5. Ladle half of the tomato sauce into a shallow ovenproof dish and spread out to cover the base. Add half the vegetable mixture, spreading it evenly. Top with about one-third of the white sauce, then about half the lasagne sheets, breaking them to fit the dish. Repeat these layers, then top with the remaining white sauce.

7 Bake for 30–45 minutes, until the top is bubbling and golden and the lasagne is tender. Garnish with fresh oregano leaves.

NUTRITIONAL INFORMATION: Energy 477kcal/2007kJ; Protein 14.5g; Carbohydrate 66.8g, of which sugars 11.6g; Fat 18.8g, of which saturates 2.7g; Cholesterol 5mg; Calcium 85mg; Fibre 9.1g; Sodium 219mg.

GARGANELLI WITH ALMOND CREAM RAGÙ

This Italian pasta dish has a wine, lemon and almond cream sauce and can be made with any white meat, such as turkey or pork fillet (tenderloin).

30ml/2 tbsp olive oil
1 onion, chopped
1 celery stick, chopped
400g/14oz boned chicken, cubed
juice and grated rind of ½ lemon,
    plus extra grated rind, to garnish
250ml/8fl oz/1 cup dry white wine
175ml/6fl oz/¾ cup well-flavoured
    chicken stock
salt and ground black pepper,
    to taste
400g/14oz garganelli
30ml/2 tbsp chopped fresh parsley
175ml/6fl oz/¾ cup almond cream

Serves 4

1 Heat the olive oil in a frying pan, add the onion and celery, and fry together gently for 10 minutes, or until soft.

2 Add the chicken and cook, stirring, to brown the meat gently all over.

3 Add the lemon juice and rind. Stir together and add the white wine. Boil hard for 30–35 minutes to evaporate the alcohol, then reduce the heat.

4 Add the chicken stock, season to taste and simmer, stirring frequently and adding extra stock if necessary, for 1 hour, until the meat is tender.

5 Meanwhile, cook the garganelli in salted boiling water according to the packet instructions.

6 Add 15ml/1 tbsp parsley and the almond cream and stir until blended. Heat until hot, then stir in the garganelli. Spoon into bowls and garnish with lemon rind and the remaining parsley.

NUTRITIONAL INFORMATION:
Energy 803kcal/3386kJ; Protein
45.1g; Carbohydrate 77.7g, of
which sugars 6g; Fat 30.6g, of
which saturates 4g; Cholesterol
70mg; Calcium 57mg; Fibre 4.9g;
Sodium 276mg.

SICHUAN NOODLES WITH SESAME SAUCE

This is traditional Chinese street food at its best; delicious egg noodles with fresh vegetables cooked in a sauce based on distinctive toasted sesame butter.

450g/1lb fresh or 225g/8oz dried
   egg noodles
½ cucumber, sliced lengthways,
   seeded and diced
4–6 spring onions (scallions), cut
   into fine shreds
bunch of radishes, about 115g/4oz,
   halved and cut into slices
225g/8oz mooli (daikon), peeled
   and grated
115g/4oz/2 cups beansprouts,
   rinsed then left in iced water
   and drained
60ml/4 tbsp groundnut (peanut) oil
   or sunflower oil
2 garlic cloves, crushed
45ml/3 tbsp toasted sesame seed
   butter, for recipe see page 49
15ml/1 tbsp sesame oil
15ml/1 tbsp light soy sauce
5–10ml/1–2 tsp chilli sauce,
   to taste
15ml/1 tbsp rice vinegar
120ml/4fl oz/½ cup chicken stock
   or water
5ml/1 tsp sugar, or to taste
salt and ground black pepper,
   to taste
roasted unsalted peanuts or
   cashew nuts, to garnish

Serves 3–4

NUTRITIONAL INFORMATION:
Energy 440kcal/1838kJ; Protein
11g; Carbohydrate 44.6g, of which
sugars 4.6g; Fat 25.4g, of which
saturates 4.1g; Cholesterol 17mg;
Calcium 128mg; Fibre 4.2g;
Sodium 384mg.

1 If using fresh noodles, cook them in boiling water for 1 minute then drain well. Rinse the noodles in fresh water and drain again. Cook dried noodles according to the instructions on the packet, draining and rinsing them as for fresh noodles.

2 Sprinkle the cucumber with salt, leave for 15 minutes, rinse well, then drain and pat dry on kitchen paper. Place in a large salad bowl. Add all the prepared spring onions, radishes, mooli and beansprouts to the cucumber and toss gently.

3 Heat half the oil in a wok or frying pan and stir-fry the noodles for about 1 minute. Transfer to a serving bowl and keep warm.

4 Heat the remaining oil in the wok, then stir-fry the garlic for 1–2 minutes. Remove from the heat and stir in the sesame seed butter, with the sesame oil, soy and chilli sauces, vinegar and stock or water. Add a little sugar and season to taste. Warm the sauce through gently. Do not overheat or the sauce will thicken too much.

5 Mix together the sauce and the noodles. Garnish with peanuts or cashew nuts and serve with the vegetables.

BEAN CHILLI WITH ALMOND MILK CORNBREAD TOPPING

This is a filling one-pot meal that needs no accompaniment. Use unstrained almond milk in the cornbread topping to add maximum flavour and protein to the dish.

115g/4oz/generous ½ cup dried red
   kidney beans, soaked overnight
115g/4oz/generous ½ cup dried
   black-eyed beans (peas),
   soaked overnight
1 bay leaf
15ml/1 tbsp vegetable oil
1 large onion, finely chopped
1 garlic clove, crushed
5ml/1 tsp ground cumin
5ml/1 tsp chilli powder
5ml/1 tsp mild paprika
2.5ml/½ tsp dried marjoram
450g/1lb mixed vegetables such as
   potatoes, carrots, aubergines
   (eggplant), parsnips and celery
1 vegetable stock (bouillon) cube
400g/14oz can chopped tomatoes
15ml/1 tbsp tomato purée (paste)
salt and ground black pepper

FOR THE CORNBREAD TOPPING
250g/9oz/2¼ cups fine cornmeal
30ml/2 tbsp wholemeal
   (whole-wheat) flour
7.5ml/1½ tsp baking powder
pinch of salt
1 egg, plus 1 egg yolk, beaten
300ml/½ pint/1¼ cups unstrained
   almond milk

Serves 4

....

NUTRITIONAL INFORMATION:
Energy 273kcal/1151kJ; Protein
16.1g; Carbohydrate 44.2g, of
which sugars 16.6g; Fat 4.8g, of
which saturates 0.7g; Cholesterol
0mg; Calcium 122mg; Fibre 17.9g;
Sodium 300mg.
....

1 Drain and rinse all the beans, then place in a pan with 600ml/ 1 pint/2½ cups cold water and the bay leaf. Boil rapidly for 10 minutes. Lower the heat, cover and simmer for 20 minutes.

2 Meanwhile, heat the oil in a large pan, add the onion and cook for 7–8 minutes. Add the garlic, cumin, chilli powder, paprika and majoram and cook for 1 minute. Add the beans and their liquid to the pan. Turn down the heat to the lowest setting, cover and simmer for 10 minutes.

3 Cut the vegetables into 2cm/¾in chunks. Add to the onion and bean mixture, making sure the potatoes and parsnips are submerged. Cover with the lid and simmer for 15 minutes or until the vegetables are almost tender.

4 Crumble the stock cube into a jug or pitcher and ladle over some of the hot cooking liquid. Stir to dissolve then add to the mixture with the tomatoes and tomato purée. Mix, then transfer the vegetable and bean mixture to an ovenproof baking dish.

5 Preheat the oven to 200°C/400°F/Gas 6. For the topping, combine the cornmeal, flour, baking powder and salt in a bowl and mix together. Make a well in the middle and add the egg and almond milk. Mix and pour over the bean mixture. Bake for 20–25 minutes, until firm and brown.

LEEK AND HAZELNUT MILK TART

For this tart a crisp hazelnut pastry case is filled with tender leeks and tofu baked in a hazelnut-milk custard. Serve warm or cold with a tomato and red onion salad.

115g/4oz/½ cup hard baking margarine, at room temperature
25ml/1½ tbsp smooth hazelnut butter
175g/6oz/1½ cups plain (all-purpose) flour
350g/12oz/3 cups leeks, thinly sliced
15ml/1 tbsp olive oil
5 eggs, lightly beaten
400ml/14fl oz/1⅔ cups full-bodied hazelnut milk
15ml/1 tbsp wholegrain mustard
salt and ground black pepper, to taste
250g/9oz firm silken tofu, drained and crumbled

Serves 6

NUTRITIONAL INFORMATION:
Energy 575kcal/2395kJ; Protein 29.8g; Carbohydrate 38.5g, of which sugars 4g; Fat 35.5g, of which saturates 5.4g; Cholesterol 193mg; Calcium 228mg; Fibre 3.2g; Sodium 243mg.

1 Put the margarine and hazelnut butter in a bowl and blend together. Transfer the paste to a piece of baking parchment and chill for 30 minutes (or freeze for 10 minutes), until hardened.

2 Sift the flour into a bowl, add the hazelnut margarine and rub it into the flour, until the mixture resembles breadcrumbs. Sprinkle over 30ml/2 tbsp cold water, mix until the crumbs begin to stick together, then gather the mixture into a ball.

3 Roll out the pastry and line a 25cm/10in flan tin (pan). Chill for 10–25 minutes, or until required.

4 Put a baking sheet in the oven and preheat it to 200°C/400°F/ Gas 6. Sweat the leeks in the oil for 10 minutes, until soft.

5 Prick the base of the pastry case and line with baking parchment and dried beans. Put on to the hot baking sheet and cook for 10 minutes. Remove the paper and beans and brush the pastry with a little of the beaten egg. Return to the oven for 4 minutes.

6 Mix together the remaining eggs with the hazelnut milk, mustard and seasoning. Stir into the leeks with the tofu and pour into the pastry case. Put into the hot oven and bake for about 30 minutes, until set and golden.

FISH IN CREAMY ALMOND SAUCE

Making a curry with an almond purée is a classic style of Indian cooking that was passed down from the Mughals; this recipe is a healthy dairy-free version.

675g/1½lb firm white fish fillets, such as tilapia, sole, monkfish or turbot, skinned and bones removed
30ml/2 tbsp lemon juice
5ml/1 tsp salt, or to taste
large pinch of saffron, pounded
30ml/2 tbsp hot almond milk
50g/2oz/¼ cup smooth almond butter
45ml/3 tbsp sunflower or light olive oil
4 green cardamom pods, bruised
2 cloves
1 bay leaf
1 large onion, finely chopped
2 cloves garlic, crushed, or 10ml/2 tsp garlic purée
2.5cm/1in fresh root ginger, grated, or 10ml/2 tsp ginger purée
2.5–5ml/½–1 tsp chilli powder
fine strips of red and green chillies, to garnish
steamed basmati rice or pilau rice, to serve

Serves 4

1 Cut the fish into 5cm/2in pieces. Sprinkle with lemon juice and salt and place in a dish. Cover and chill for 20 minutes.

2 Crumble the saffron into a bowl and pour over the hot milk. Leave to soak for 15 minutes. Put the almond butter in a jug or pitcher and gradually blend in 150ml/¼ pint/⅔ cup boiling water to make a thin almond purée with the consistency of single (light) cream. Combine with the saffron milk and set aside.

3 Heat the oil in a heavy frying pan, until hot. Add the cardamom, cloves and bay leaf to the pan. Cook for about a minute, until the cardamom pods puff up. Add the onion and increase the heat to medium. Fry until soft but not brown, stirring frequently. Add the garlic and ginger and continue to fry for about 1 minute.

4 Stir in the chilli powder, then pour in 200ml/7fl oz/scant 1 cup hot water. Stir, then add the fish in a single layer. Reduce the heat to low and cook for 2–3 minutes. Pour the almond purée over the fish, mix gently and simmer for 3–4 minutes, until the sauce has thickened slightly.

5 Remove from the heat and transfer to a warmed serving dish. Garnish with fine strips of red and green chilli and serve with steamed basmati rice or pilau rice.

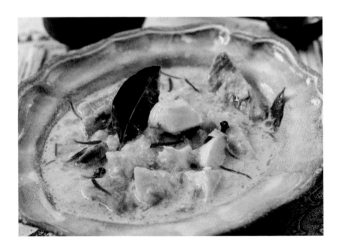

NUTRITIONAL INFORMATION:
Energy 320kcal/1336kJ; Protein 34.8g; Carbohydrate 7.4g, of which sugars 3.3g; Fat 17.6g, of which saturates 2.1g; Cholesterol 78mg; Calcium 30mg; Fibre 3.3g; Sodium 104mg.

PRAWNS IN A POPPY SEED AND CASHEW NUT SAUCE

Briefly marinating the prawns starts the cooking process; they are then braised in a rich sauce, thickened with cashew nut butter, for just a few minutes.

500g/14lb raw tiger prawns
(jumbo shrimp), peeled and
deveined (see Cook's tip)
45ml/3 tbsp lemon juice
2.5ml/½ tsp ground turmeric
50g/2oz/¼ cup smooth cashew
nut butter
30ml/2 tbsp white poppy seeds
60ml/4 tbsp sunflower or light
olive oil
1 large onion, finely chopped
2.5cm/1in fresh root ginger, grated,
or 10ml/2 tsp ginger purée
2 cloves garlic, crushed or
10ml/2 tsp garlic purée
1–3 fresh green chillies, finely
chopped (seeded if preferred)
2.5–5ml/½–1 tsp chilli powder
5ml/1 tsp salt, or to taste
200ml/7fl oz/scant 1 cup boiling
water or vegetable stock
fine strips of fresh red and green
chillies, to garnish

Serves 4

Cook's tip
To devein prawns (shrimp):
locate the black vein that
runs along the back of the
prawn and make a slit either
side of it. Remove the vein
with the tip of the knife.

NUTRITIONAL INFORMATION:
Energy 207kcal/859kJ; Protein 5.5g;
Carbohydrate 8.7g, of which sugars
3.9g; Fat 17.5g, of which saturates
2.9g; Cholesterol 24mg; Calcium
27mg; Fibre 1.2g; Sodium 27mg.

1 Mix the prawns, lemon juice and turmeric together in a bowl. Set aside for 15 minutes.

2 Put the cashew nut butter in a jug or pitcher and gradually blend in 150ml/¼ pint/⅔ cup boiling water to make a thin cashew nut purée with the consistency of single (light) cream.

3 Preheat a small, heavy pan over a medium heat and dry-roast the poppy seeds until they begin to crackle. Remove from the heat, leave to cool, then grind the seeds in a coffee grinder.

4 Heat the oil in a heavy pan over a medium heat, add the onion and fry for 5 minutes, until it is soft but not brown. Add the ginger, garlic and green chillies. Cook for 2–3 minutes, then add the chilli powder and salt. Stir and cook gently for 2 minutes. Pour in the boiling water or vegetable stock. Reduce the heat to low, cover the pan and cook for 2–3 minutes.

5 Add the prawns and cashew nut butter mixture with the poppy seeds. Stir well and simmer, uncovered, for 3–4 minutes or until the prawns are cooked and the sauce slightly thickened.

6 Ladle the prawns and some of the sauce into warmed serving bowls and serve garnished with fine strips of chilli.

TURKEY WITH WALNUT SAUCE

Turkey is gently poached to keep it moist, then cut into chunks. The thick sauce is relatively low in fat and is created from a purée of onions, garlic and walnut butter.

500g/1¼lb skinned turkey
    breast fillet
500ml/17fl oz/generous 2 cups
    water
2.5ml/½ tsp salt
15ml/1 tbsp sunflower oil
2 onions, chopped
2 garlic cloves, finely chopped
30ml/2 tbsp walnut butter
5ml/1 tsp ground coriander
pinch of cayenne pepper
raw unsalted walnut halves
    (optional) and fresh coriander
    (cilantro) leaves, to garnish

Serves 6

Variations
• Substitute chicken breast fillets for the turkey.
• Add some chopped fresh coriander (cilantro) to the sauce if you like.
• This recipe is also delicious made with hazelnut butter.
• Add some chopped fresh parsley to the sauce and garnish the dish with sprigs of flat leaf parsley.

1 Put the turkey in a medium pan and pour over enough of the cold water to cover. Bring to the boil, reduce the heat and simmer for 5 minutes, skimming the surface if necessary. Add the salt, cover and cook for a further 15 minutes. Drain and set aside, retaining the poaching liquid.

2 Heat the oil in a frying pan. Add the onions and garlic. Fry for 5 minutes, until softened but not browned, then transfer the mixture to a food processor.

3 Add the walnut butter, ground coriander and cayenne pepper and half of the poaching liquid from the turkey. Process until smooth. Add more liquid, a little at a time, until you achieve a sauce-like consistency. Transfer to a large bowl.

4 Cut the turkey into 3cm/1¼in chunks. Add to the sauce and stir until the turkey is coated. Cover and chill overnight. To serve, turn the turkey into a serving dish. Garnish with walnut halves, if you wish, and coriander leaves.

....

NUTRITIONAL INFORMATION:
Energy 160kcal/673kJ; Protein 21.8g; Carbohydrate 6.9g, of which sugars 3.7g; Fat 5.5g, of which saturates 1.1g; Cholesterol 58mg; Calcium 22mg; Fibre 1.3g; Sodium 216mg.
....

TURKEY IN A COCONUT AND CASHEW NUT SAUCE

There are many versions of korma; some use ground almonds, others dairy cream. This one is based on cashew nut yogurt and coconut milk and is rich but not cloying.

200g/7oz/¾ cup cashew nut yogurt
10ml/2 tsp gram flour
10ml/2 tsp ginger purée
10ml/2 tsp garlic purée
2.5ml/½ tsp ground turmeric
2.5–5ml/½–1 tsp chilli powder
5ml/1 tsp salt, or to taste
675g/1½lb skinned turkey breast
   fillet, cut into 5cm/2in cubes
75ml/6 tbsp vegetable oil
2.5cm/1in piece of cinnamon stick
6 green cardamom pods, bruised
6 cloves
2 bay leaves
1 large onion, finely chopped
15ml/1 tbsp sesame seeds,
   finely ground
200ml/7fl oz/¾ cup coconut milk
50g/2oz/½ cup raw unsalted
   cashew nuts, soaked in 150ml/
   ¼ pint/⅔ cup boiling water for
   20 minutes
1.5ml/¼ tsp freshly grated nutmeg
1.5ml/¼ tsp ground mace
boiled rice, to serve

Serves 4

1 Whisk the cashew nut yogurt and gram flour together until smooth (do this thoroughly, otherwise the yogurt will curdle). Stir in the ginger, garlic, turmeric, chilli powder and salt. Pour the marinade over the turkey. Stir to coat. Cover and leave for 30 minutes.

2 Reserve 5ml/1 tsp of oil and heat the remainder in a pan over a low heat. Add the cinnamon, cardamom, cloves and bay leaves. Let these sizzle until the cardamom pods have puffed up. Add the onion and increase the heat slightly. Sauté for 5 minutes until translucent, then stir in the ground sesame seeds.

3 Add the marinated turkey, increase the heat to medium-high and cook for about 5 minutes, until the turkey changes colour. Pour in the coconut milk and 150ml/¼ pint/⅔ cup warm water. Bring this to the boil, reduce the heat to low, cover and simmer for 20 minutes or until the turkey is tender.

4 Purée the cashews with their soaking water. Add to the turkey. Simmer, uncovered, for 5–6 minutes, until the sauce thickens.

5 Heat the reserved oil in a small pan. Add the nutmeg and mace, then cook gently for about 30 seconds. Mix the spiced oil with the turkey. Serve with boiled rice.

NUTRITIONAL INFORMATION:
Energy 504kcal/2104kJ; Protein 44.7g; Carbohydrate 16.2g, of which sugars 8.3g; Fat 29.3g, of which saturates 4.1g; Cholesterol 118mg; Calcium 55mg; Fibre 2.1g; Sodium 313mg.

CHICKEN FRICASSÉE WITH ALMOND BUTTER

This country-style meal has onions and mushrooms in a creamy white wine and almond butter sauce, perfect for those with lactose or dairy intolerance.

20 small even-size button (pearl)
    onions or shallots
60ml/4 tbsp sunflower oil
1.2–1.3kg/2½–3lb chicken, cut into
    pieces
45ml/3 tbsp plain (all-purpose) flour
250ml/8fl oz/1 cup dry white wine
600ml/1 pint/2½ cups boiling
    chicken stock
1 bouquet garni
5ml/1 tsp lemon juice
salt and ground black pepper,
    to taste
225g/8oz/3 cups button (white)
    mushrooms
30ml/2 tbsp smooth almond butter
45ml/3 tbsp chopped fresh parsley,
    to garnish

Serves 4

Cook's tips
• To test that the chicken is cooked, pierce the thickest part of one of the portions with a skewer or thin knife; the juices should run clear.
• A bouquet garni is made up of parsley stalks, a sprig of thyme and a bay leaf. Tie with a piece of string.

NUTRITIONAL INFORMATION:
Energy 686kcal/2849kJ; Protein 45g; Carbohydrate 15.5g, of which sugars 3.8g; Fat 45.6g, of which saturates 10.1g; Cholesterol 215mg; Calcium 52mg; Fibre 3.8g; Sodium 154mg.

1 Preheat the oven to 180°C/350°F/Gas 4. Put the onions or shallots in a bowl, cover with boiling water and leave to soak.

2 Heat half the oil in a large frying pan. Add the chicken and cook on a high heat, turning occasionally, until browned all over. Transfer to a large casserole, leaving the juices behind.

3 Stir the flour into the pan juices, then blend in the wine. Stir in the stock and add the bouquet garni and lemon juice. Bring to the boil, stirring, until thickened. Season and pour over the chicken. Cover the casserole and put in the oven. Cook for 1 hour.

4 Drain and peel the onions or shallots. Trim the stalks from the mushrooms. Clean the frying pan, then add the remaining oil. Add the mushrooms and onions or shallots and cook for 5 minutes, turning, until lightly browned. Add to the chicken.

5 Cook for 1 hour, until the chicken is cooked. Remove the chicken and vegetables to a warmed dish. Whisk the almond butter and 30ml/2 tbsp parsley into the sauce. Check the seasoning, then pour the sauce over the chicken. Garnish with parsley.

APRICOT AND ALMOND BUTTER STUFFED CHICKEN

Couscous makes a delicious, simple base for this sweet-and-sour stuffing flavoured with apricots and crunchy almond butter. This is an elegant dish for a special occasion.

4 skinned boneless chicken breast portions
50g/2oz/⅓ cup instant couscous
150ml/¼ pint/⅔ cup boiling chicken stock
30ml/2 tbsp crunchy almond butter
50g/2oz/¼ cup dried apricots soaked for 1 hour in 150ml/¼ pint/⅔ cup orange juice
1.5ml/¼ tsp dried tarragon
salt and ground black pepper
1 egg yolk
30ml/2 tbsp orange marmalade
boiled or steamed basmati and wild rice, to serve

Serves 4

Variation
For date and walnut-stuffed chicken, use dried unsugared dates instead of apricots, and walnut butter instead of almond butter. Add 15ml/1 tbsp chopped fresh coriander (cilantro) or parsley instead of the dried tarragon.

Cook's tip
Don't forget to remove the cocktail sticks (toothpicks) before serving.

NUTRITIONAL INFORMATION:
Energy 299kcal/1263kJ; Protein 39.9g; Carbohydrate 18.8g, of which sugars 10.6g; Fat 8.1g, of which saturates 1.4g; Cholesterol 155mg; Calcium 29mg; Fibre 2.8g; Sodium 104mg.

1 Cut a deep pocket horizontally in each chicken breast portion, without cutting all the way through. Put the chicken between two sheets of oiled baking parchment or clear film (plastic wrap), then gently beat with a rolling pin until slightly thinner.

2 Put the couscous in a bowl and add 60ml/4 tbsp of the stock. Add the almond butter and stir until mixed. Leave to stand for 5 minutes to allow the couscous to soak up the liquid. Drain the apricots, reserving the juice, then stir them into the couscous with the tarragon. Season, then stir in just enough egg yolk to bind the mixture together.

3 Divide the stuffing between the chicken portions, packing it firmly into the pockets, then securing with wooden cocktail sticks (toothpicks). Place the chicken portions in a pan in which they fit close together but not too tightly.

4 Stir the marmalade into the remaining hot stock until dissolved, then stir in the reserved orange juice. Season and pour over the chicken. Cover and slowly bring to the boil. Reduce the heat and simmer for 25 minutes, until the chicken is cooked through.

5 Remove the chicken and keep it warm. Boil the sauce remaining in the pan until it is reduced by half. Carve the chicken into slices and arrange on serving plates. Spoon over the sauce and serve immediately with basmati and wild rice.

CHICKEN, PORK AND POTATOES IN PEANUT SAUCE

This Peruvian dish is usually made with dried potatoes, which break up when cooked to thicken the sauce. Sliced floury potatoes, used here, work equally well.

60ml/4 tbsp olive oil
3 chicken breast portions, halved
salt and ground black pepper,
    to taste
500g/1¼lb boneless pork loin,
    cut into 2cm/¾in pieces
1 large onion, chopped
30–45ml/2–3 tbsp water
3 garlic cloves, crushed
5ml/1 tsp paprika
5ml/1 tsp ground cumin
500g/1¼lb floury potatoes, peeled
    and thickly sliced
30ml/2 tbsp smooth peanut butter
550ml/18fl oz/scant 2½ cups
    vegetable stock
2 hard-boiled eggs, sliced,
    50g/2oz/½ cup pitted black
    olives, and chopped fresh flat
    leaf parsley, to garnish
cooked rice, to serve

Serves 6

Variation
Other nut butters, such as almond or hazelnut butter, would also work well in this hearty dish.

NUTRITIONAL INFORMATION:
Energy 259kcal/1083kJ; Protein 21.5g; Carbohydrate 18.3g, of which sugars 3.8g; Fat 11.6g, of which saturates 2.1g; Cholesterol 80mg; Calcium 26mg; Fibre 1.9g; Sodium 214mg.

1 Heat half the olive oil in a heavy pan over a medium-high heat. Add the chicken breast portions, season and cook for 10 minutes, until golden brown all over. Transfer the pieces of chicken to a plate, using a slotted spoon.

2 Heat the remaining oil in the pan. When it is very hot, add the pork. Season and sauté for 3–4 minutes, until golden brown. Transfer to the plate containing the chicken pieces.

3 Lower the heat and stir the onion into the oil in the pan. Cook for 5 minutes, adding the water if it begins to stick. Stir in the garlic, paprika and cumin and cook for 1 minute more. Add the potatoes, stir and cover. Cook for 3 minutes.

4 Blend the peanut butter with a little of the stock until smooth, then stir into the rest of the stock. Add to the pan, bring to the boil and simmer for 20 minutes.

5 Return the chicken and pork to the pan and bring the mixture to the boil. Lower the heat, cover the pan and simmer the stew for 6–8 minutes, until the meat is just cooked. Serve immediately, garnished with the sliced hard-boiled egg, black olives and chopped parsley, and with rice to accompany it.

PORK AND PINEAPPLE COCONUT MILK CURRY

The heat of this colourful curry balances out its sweetness to make a fragrant dish.
It takes very little time to cook, so is ideal for a quick and tasty meal.

400ml/14fl oz/1⅔ cups reduced-fat
coconut milk
10ml/2 tsp Thai red curry paste
400g/14oz lean pork loin steaks,
trimmed and thinly sliced
15ml/1 tbsp Thai fish sauce
5ml/1 tsp palm sugar or light
muscovado (brown) sugar
15ml/1 tbsp tamarind juice, made
by mixing tamarind paste with
warm water
2 kaffir lime leaves, torn
½ medium pineapple, peeled,
cored and chopped
1 fresh red chilli, seeded and
thinly sliced (optional),
to garnish

Serves 4

NUTRITIONAL INFORMATION:
Energy 199kcal/845kJ; Protein
22.9g; Carbohydrate 16.8g, of
which sugars 16.7g; Fat 5.1g, of
which saturates 1.6g; Cholesterol
63mg; Calcium 60mg; Fibre 1.6g;
Sodium 481mg.

1 Pour the coconut milk into a bowl and let it settle, so that the
cream rises to the surface. Scoop the cream into a measuring jug
(cup). You should have about 250ml/8fl oz/1 cup. If necessary,
add a little of the coconut milk to make up the volume.

2 Pour the coconut cream into a large pan and bring it to the
boil. Cook the coconut cream for about 10 minutes, or until
the cream separates, stirring frequently to prevent it from
sticking to the base of the pan and scorching.

3 Add the red curry paste and stir until well mixed. Cook, stirring
occasionally, for about 4 minutes, until the paste is fragrant.

4 Add the sliced pork and stir in the fish sauce, sugar and
tamarind juice. Cook, stirring constantly, for 1–2 minutes, until
the sugar has dissolved and the pork is no longer pink.

5 Add the remaining coconut milk and the lime leaves. Bring to
the boil, then stir in the pineapple. Reduce the heat and simmer
gently for 3 minutes, or until the pork is fully cooked. Ladle into
bowls, garnish with the sliced chilli, if using, and serve.

PORK STEAK WITH ALMOND STUFFING

This is an excellent way to use almond pulp after making almond milk and makes a lighter-textured stuffing than one made with breadcrumbs.

2 evenly sized pork steaks, about
    400g/14oz each
115g/4oz/1 cup dried almond flour
30ml/2 tbsp almond butter
small bunch of parsley and thyme,
    leaves chopped
1 onion, chopped
1 egg, lightly beaten
finely grated rind and juice of
    1 small orange
salt and ground black pepper,
    to taste
15ml/1 tbsp olive oil
steamed cabbage, to serve

Serves 6

Cook's tip
Make a gravy by thickening
the meat juices with a little
flour. Add the reserved orange
juice and heat through.

NUTRITIONAL INFORMATION:
Energy 233kcal/974kJ; Protein
18.7g; Carbohydrate 19.3g, of
which sugars 2.2g; Fat 9.1g, of
which saturates 1.9g; Cholesterol
81mg; Calcium 29mg; Fibre 2.2g;
Sodium 60mg.

1 Preheat the oven to 180°C/350°F/Gas 4. Slit the pork steaks lengthways; do not cut right through. Hold out each of the flaps and slit them lengthways in the same way. Flatten out gently.

2 Put the dried almond flour, almond butter, herbs, onion, egg, orange rind and seasoning in a bowl. Mix with a fork, including as much of the orange juice as is required to bind the stuffing.

3 To cook the steaks individually, divide the stuffing in half and lay it down the centre of each; fold the flaps up towards the middle and secure with cotton string or skewers to make a roll. Alternatively, turn all the stuffing on to one of the fillets, spread evenly, then cover with the second fillet.

4 Rub the pork fillets with olive oil. Season with salt and pepper and put into a shallow dish or roasting pan with 300ml/½ pint/ 1¼ cups water to prevent the meat from drying out.

5 Cover the dish and cook in the oven for 50 minutes–1 hour, turning and basting after 30 minutes. Allow the meat to rest for 10 minutes, then slice and serve with steamed cabbage.

THAI BEEF CURRY IN SWEET PEANUT SAUCE

In this classic dish from Thailand, beef is slow-cooked with aromatic ingredients until tender, then peanut butter is used to thicken the juices, yielding a rich, glossy sauce.

600ml/1 pint/2½ cups coconut milk
45ml/3 tbsp Thai red curry paste
45ml/3 tbsp Thai fish sauce
30ml/2 tbsp palm sugar or light
 muscovado (brown) sugar
2 lemon grass stalks, bruised
450g/1lb rump (round) steak,
 cut into thin strips
75ml/5 tbsp crunchy peanut butter
2 fresh red chillies, sliced
5 kaffir lime leaves, torn
salt and ground black pepper,
 to taste
2 salted eggs, cut in wedges,
 and 10–15 Thai basil leaves,
 to garnish

Serves 4–6

Cook's tips
• Store-bought Thai red curry paste can vary in heat, so it is worth starting with a small amount and adding more only as required.
• Eggs are salted in Thailand as a way of preserving them, and lend a contrasting salty note to the sweetness of this curry. Be aware that the longer they are kept, the saltier the eggs become.

NUTRITIONAL INFORMATION:
Energy 310kcal/1296kJ; Protein 29.1g; Carbohydrate 9.7g, of which sugars 8.5g; Fat 17.4g, of which saturates 5.3g; Cholesterol 69mg; Calcium 59mg; Fibre 1.2g; Sodium 215mg.

1 Pour half the coconut milk into a large, heavy pan. Place over a medium heat and bring to the boil, stirring constantly for about 10 minutes, until the milk separates.

2 Stir in the red curry paste and cook for 2–3 minutes until the mixture is fragrant and thoroughly blended. Add the fish sauce, sugar and bruised lemon grass stalks. Mix well.

3 Continue to cook until the colour deepens. Gradually add the remaining coconut milk, stirring constantly. Bring the mixture back to the boil.

4 Add the beef and crunchy peanut butter. Cook, stirring constantly, for 8–10 minutes, or until most of the liquid has evaporated. Add the chillies and kaffir lime leaves. Season to taste and serve, garnished with wedges of salted eggs and Thai basil leaves.

LAMB IN ROSE-SCENTED ALMOND SAUCE

This recipe is typical of the elegant and rich, creamy dishes brought to India by the Mughals, and it offers us a delicious way of using nut milk and butter. A sprinkling of rose water adds a delicate aroma to tender slices of braised lamb.

large pinch of saffron threads, lightly pounded
30ml/2 tbsp hot almond milk
25g/1oz/¼ cup raw unsalted blanched almonds
675g/1½lb boned leg of lamb
75ml/5 tbsp almond milk yogurt
10ml/2 tsp gram flour
60ml/4 tbsp sunflower oil or light olive oil
1 large onion, finely chopped
2 fresh green chillies, seeded and finely chopped
2.5ml/1in fresh root ginger, grated, or 10ml/2 tsp ginger purée
2 cloves garlic, crushed, or 10ml/ 2 tsp garlic purée
2.5ml/½ tsp ground turmeric
10ml/2 tsp ground cumin
5ml/1 tsp ground coriander
2.5–5ml/½–1 tsp chilli powder
5ml/1 tsp salt, or to taste
30ml/2 tbsp almond butter
2.5ml/½ tsp garam masala
30ml/2 tbsp rose water
toasted flaked (sliced) almonds, to garnish
pilau rice, to serve

Serves 4

Cook's tip
The flavour of this curry improves if it is allowed to cool before being covered and chilled overnight, then reheated the next day and served piping hot. It also freezes very well.

1 Crumble the saffron into a small bowl. Pour over the hot almond milk and leave to soak.

2 Put the almonds in another bowl and pour over 150ml/¼ pint/ ⅔ cup boiling water. Leave for 20 minutes. Purée the almonds with their liquid in a blender, until smooth.

3 Trim any fat from the lamb, then place it on a chopping board and cover it with baking parchment. Gently bash it with a wooden rolling pin to flatten the meat until it is 5mm/¼in thick. Cut the lamb into thin slices, about 2.5cm/1in long.

4 Mix together the almond milk yogurt and gram flour in a small bowl, until smooth.

5 Heat the oil in a heavy frying pan over a medium heat, add the onion and fry until soft, but not brown, stirring frequently. Add the green chillies, ginger and garlic and cook for 2 minutes, then add the dry spices and cook for 1 minute, stirring.

6 Add the meat to the pan and cook, stirring, for 1–2 minutes, until it is lightly browned. Stir in the almond milk yogurt and flour mixture and cook, stirring, for a further 2–3 minutes, until most of the moisture evaporates and the fat separates from the spice paste. Pour in 150ml/¼ pint/⅔ cup hot water and season with salt. Bring to the boil, cover and reduce the heat to low.

7 Cook, stirring occasionally for 35 minutes. Blend the almond butter with 60ml/4 tbsp boiling water. Add to the pan with the almond purée and the saffron with its soaking liquid. Cover and simmer for a further 10–12 minutes or until the meat is tender. Stir in the garam masala and rose water.

8 Transfer to a warmed serving dish or individual plates, garnish with toasted almonds and serve with pilau rice.

NUTRITIONAL INFORMATION: Energy 547kcal/2277kJ; Protein 38.2g; Carbohydrate 12.1g, of which sugars 4.7g; Fat 39.2g, of which saturates 11g; Cholesterol 128mg; Calcium 51mg; Fibre 2.9g; Sodium 161mg.

DESSERTS

COCONUT MILK ICE CREAM

This creamy coconut and lime ice cream is bliss on sultry days and particularly welcome as a cooling dessert to follow a hot and spicy main meal.

150ml/¼ pint/⅔ cup water
115g/4oz/½ cup caster
   (superfine) sugar
2 limes
400ml/14fl oz/1⅔ cups coconut
   milk
toasted coconut shavings,
   to garnish (see Cook's tips)

Serves 4–6

Cook's tips
• For the garnish, spread out some flaked coconut on a baking sheet lined with a piece of baking parchment and bake at 150°C/300°F/ Gas 2 for 12–15 minutes, turning every few minutes so that the coconut colours evenly, until golden brown. Keep a close eye on it as coconut burns easily. Cool before using.
• Make sure you use full-fat and not reduced-fat coconut milk for this ice cream.

1 Put the water in a small pan. Tip in the caster sugar and bring to the boil, stirring constantly until it has all dissolved. Remove the pan from the heat and leave the syrup to cool, then chill well.

2 Grate the limes finely, taking care to avoid the bitter pith. Squeeze them and pour the juice and rind into the pan of syrup. Add the coconut milk.

3 Churn the mixture in an ice-cream maker until it is firm enough to scoop. If you don't have an ice-cream maker, pour the mixture into a suitable freezer container and freeze it for 1½ hours, or until the sides and base are just frozen and the middle is a soft slush. Beat using an electric whisk for 30 seconds. Quickly return it to the freezer and repeat twice more at hourly intervals, then freeze for at least 2 hours.

4 Serve the ice cream in chilled bowls or glasses, decorated with a few toasted coconut shavings or fine strips of lime rind.

NUTRITIONAL INFORMATION:
Energy 90kcal/386kJ; Protein 0.3g; Carbohydrate 23.3g, of which sugars 23.3g; Fat 0.2g, of which saturates 0.1g; Cholesterol 0mg; Calcium 25mg; Fibre 0g; Sodium 74mg.

ALMOND MILK AND PISTACHIO MILK ICE CREAMS

Full-bodied nut milks make rich ice creams, so should be served in small portions.
Make them with unstrained nut milks so that you get flecks of nut in the mixture.

FOR THE ALMOND MILK
ICE CREAM
600ml/1 pint/2½ cups full-bodied
  unstrained almond milk
4 egg yolks
150g/5oz/¾ cup caster (superfine)
  sugar
5ml/1 tsp cornflour (cornstarch)
30–45ml/3–4 tbsp orange flower
  water
2–3 drops almond extract

FOR THE PISTACHIO MILK
ICE CREAM
600ml/1 pint/2½ cups full-bodied
  unstrained pistachio milk
4 egg yolks
150g/5oz/¾ cup caster (superfine)
  sugar
5ml/1 tsp cornflour (cornstarch)
2.5ml/½ tsp vanilla extract
2–3 drops green food colouring
  (optional)

Serves 6–8

Cook's tip
Decorate the ice cream with
slivers of raw unsalted
blanched almonds or
pistachio nuts, if you like.

NUTRITIONAL INFORMATION:
Energy 288kcal/1213kJ; Protein
5.7g; Carbohydrate 43.7g, of
which sugars 40g; Fat 11.3g, of
which saturates 2.2g; Cholesterol
202mg; Calcium 35mg; Fibre 1.9g;
Sodium 64mg.

1 To make the almond ice cream, pour the almond milk into a
heavy pan and heat until steaming hot, but do not boil.

2 Whisk the egg yolks, sugar and cornflour together in a bowl
until thick and creamy. Gradually whisk in the hot milk, then
pour back into the pan. Cook over a low heat for 10 minutes,
until the custard thickens, but do not boil. Stir in the orange
flower water and almond extract. Leave to cool.

3 Pour the mixture into a bowl or freezer container and chill,
then freeze. Whisk the mixture after about 1 hour. Continue
to freeze the ice cream, whisking two or three times, until it is
smooth and thick. Return it to the freezer and leave it for several
hours or overnight. Alternatively, churn in an ice-cream maker.

4 Make the pistachio ice cream in the same way, using the
pistachio milk instead of the almond milk and vanilla extract
instead of the almond extract. Add a little green food colouring
to the pistachio ice cream, if you like.

5 Remove the ice creams from the freezer 15 minutes before
serving to allow them to soften slightly. Serve one scoop of each
flavour per person.

ALMOND MILK AND ROSE WATER BLANCMANGE

This smooth and delicate dessert is made with almond milk, as it would have been during the Middle Ages when blancmange (literally 'white food') was a banqueting dish. This more modern version is made with gelatine to achieve a light wobbly set.

5 sheets of gelatine
1 lemon
900ml/1½ pints/3¾ full-bodied
    unstrained almond milk
115g/4oz/½ cup caster
    (superfine) sugar
30–45ml/2–3 tbsp rose water
fresh or sugared rose petals,
    to decorate (optional)

Serves 6

Cook's tip
Make sure you use
unsprayed rose petals when
decorating; those from a
florist will almost certainly
have been sprayed with
inedible chemicals.

NUTRITIONAL INFORMATION:
Energy 104kcal/443kJ; Protein 0.7g;
Carbohydrate 24.2g, of which sugars
24.2g; Fat 1.3g, of which saturates
0g; Cholesterol 0mg; Calcium 6mg;
Fibre 0g; Sodium 106mg.

1 Soak the gelatine leaves in a small bowl of cold water for about 5 minutes to soften them.

2 Thinly pare strips of rind from the lemon, taking care not to include the white pith. Heat the almond milk gently with the lemon rind until it just comes to the boil. Discard the rind.

3 Lift the softened sheets of gelatine out of the soaking water, squeezing out the excess liquid. Stir the gelatine into the hot almond milk until it has dissolved. Stir in the sugar until that too has dissolved. Add the rose water to taste and mix well.

4 Pour into one large or six individual wetted moulds. Place the mould(s) in the refrigerator and chill until completely set.

5 Turn the blancmange out of its mould(s) just before serving. Decorate with rose petals, if you like.

APPLE AND WALNUT MILK FLUMMERY

Although the name of this pudding comes from the Welsh, the Celtic countries all share this soft, sweet dessert. In Scotland it is based on oatmeal, but this Irish variation uses barley and also includes apples and walnut milk.

90ml/6 tbsp pearl barley
675g/1½lb cooking apples, peeled, cored and sliced
50g/2oz/¼ cup caster (superfine) sugar
juice of 1 lemon

FOR THE WALNUT MILK CUSTARD
250ml/8fl oz/1 cup walnut milk
2 egg yolks
5ml/1 tsp cornflour (cornstarch)
15ml/1 tbsp caster (superfine) sugar

Serves 4–6

Variation
This flummery is also good made with pears; choose large cooking ones rather than dessert pears as those will cook to a soft purée. If liked, add a handful of raspberries to the pears a few minutes before the end of cooking; they will turn the fruit purée an attractive pink colour and add a sharp taste.

NUTRITIONAL INFORMATION:
Energy 191kcal/812kJ; Protein 3.2g; Carbohydrate 36.4g, of which sugars 21.3g; Fat 4.9g, of which saturates 0.9g; Cholesterol 69mg; Calcium 19mg; Fibre 2.9g; Sodium 27mg.

1 Make the walnut custard. Pour the milk into a heavy pan and heat until it is almost boiling. Meanwhile, whisk the egg yolks, cornflour and sugar together in a bowl until thick and creamy.

2 Gradually whisk the hot milk into the egg mixture, then pour through a fine sieve (strainer) back into the pan. Cook over a low heat, stirring constantly for 10 minutes, until the custard thickens; do not allow to boil or the custard may curdle. Pour the custard back into the bowl and cover with a piece of damp baking parchment to stop a skin forming. Leave to cool.

3 Put 1 litre/1¾ pints/4 cups of water into a pan. Add the barley and bring to the boil. Add the apples to the pan and continue cooking until the barley is soft and the apples are cooked.

4 Blend the mixture, or press it through a sieve. Return it to the rinsed pan. Add the sugar and lemon juice. Bring back to the boil.

5 Remove from the heat and allow to cool. Turn into individual glasses or a serving dish. Chill. Stir in the custard and serve cold.

BAKED COFFEE CUSTARDS WITH MACADAMIA NUT CREAM

Macadamia nut milk is exceptionally rich and creamy and is perfect for these coffee custards. Whipped macadamia nut cream adds a finishing flourish.

450ml/¾ pint/scant 2 cups
  macadamia nut milk
25g/1oz ground coffee (not instant)
3 eggs
30ml/2 tbsp light muscovado
  (brown) or coconut sugar
thick macadamia nut cream
  (see page 51 and substitute
  macadamia nuts for cashew
  nuts)
raw cacao or (unsweetened) cocoa
  powder, to serve

Serves 4

Variation
For chocolate and macadamia milk custards, leave out the coffee and add 115g/4oz good-quality plain (semi-sweet) chocolate, broken into squares and 2.5ml/½ tsp vanilla extract to the hot milk (no need to strain it) in step 2. Stir until melted, then continue as per the recipe.

NUTRITIONAL INFORMATION:
Energy 152kcal/634kJ; Protein 6.3g;
Carbohydrate 8.9g, of which sugars
8.2g; Fat 10.8g, of which saturates
2.3g; Cholesterol 173mg; Calcium
28mg; Fibre 0.9g; Sodium 67mg.

1 Preheat the oven to 190°C/375°F/Gas 5. Put the macadamia nut milk in a heavy pan and bring to the boil. Add the coffee, remove from the heat and leave to infuse for 10 minutes.

2 Strain the flavoured milk into a clean pan, discarding the coffee grounds, and gently heat until just starting to simmer.

3 Beat the eggs and sugar in a bowl until pale and fluffy. Pour over the hot milk mixture, whisking constantly.

4 Pour the mixture into individual heatproof bowls or coffee cups and cover tightly with foil. Place them in a roasting pan and pour in enough boiling water to come halfway up the sides.

5 Carefully place the roasting pan in the oven. Cook the custards for about 30 minutes, or until they are set. Remove from the roasting pan and leave to cool completely. Transfer to the refrigerator and chill for at least 2 hours.

6 Just before serving, spoon over some thick macadamia nut cream and dust with raw cacao or cocoa powder.

ALMOND MILK PUDDING

This is a classic Turkish dessert and is always served in individual portions. Traditionally it is decorated with grated pistachio nuts, which add colour and flavour.

115g/4oz/1 cup raw unsalted
   blanched almonds
600ml/1 pint/2½ cups almond milk
25g/1oz rice flour
115g/4oz/generous ½ cup sugar
30ml/2 tbsp grated raw unsalted
   pistachio nuts

Serves 4

Variation
For fig and almond puddings,
cut 4 figs into pieces, put in
a bowl and drizzle with 30ml/
2 tbsp acacia honey. Make
the pudding, allow it to cool,
then divide the figs and
juices between four glasses
and spoon over the pudding.
Decorate with grated nuts
and chill before serving.

NUTRITIONAL INFORMATION:
Energy 355kcal/1487kJ; Protein 7.9g;
Carbohydrate 37.7g, of which sugars
31.7g; Fat 20.1g, of which saturates
1.8g; Cholesterol 0mg; Calcium
87mg; Fibre 0.8g; Sodium 52mg.

1 Using a mortar and pestle, food processor or nut mill, pound or grind the almonds to a paste. Blend the paste with a little of the almond milk until smooth, then set aside.

2 In a small bowl, slake the rice flour with a little almond milk to form a smooth paste, the consistency of thick cream. Set aside.

3 Pour the rest of the almond milk into a heavy pan. Add the sugar and bring the almond milk to the boil, stirring constantly. Stir 30ml/2 tbsp of the hot almond milk into the slaked rice flour and then add to the pan. Make sure you keep stirring to prevent the rice flour from cooking in clumps. Cook until the mixture coats the back of the wooden spoon.

4 Stir in the almond paste and reduce the heat. Simmer gently for about 25 minutes, stirring occasionally, until the mixture is thick. Pour into individual bowls and leave to cool.

5 Sprinkle the grated pistachio nuts over each bowl – this is often done in a thin line across the middle of the pudding – and place the bowls in the refrigerator. Serve chilled.

CHOCOLATE, COCONUT AND ALMOND TORTE

Despite its decadent appearance and deep chocolate flavour, this torte is packed with raw healthy ingredients. Coconut butter and oil are used in both the base and filling.

FOR THE BASE
50g/2oz/¼ cup coconut butter
50g/2oz/¼ cup coconut oil
30ml/2 tbsp coconut sugar or soft
    dark brown sugar
150g/5oz/1¼ cups ground almonds
150g/5oz/1⅔ cups desiccated
    (dry unsweetened shredded)
    coconut
5ml/1 tsp raw cacao or
    (unsweetened) cocoa powder

FOR THE FILLING
115g/4oz/scant 1 cup stoned
    (pitted) dates, preferably
    Medjool dates
25g/1oz/2 tbsp coconut butter
25g/1oz/2 tbsp coconut oil
150g/5oz/scant ¾ cup clear honey
115g/4oz/1 cup raw cacao or
    cocoa (unsweetened) powder
finely grated rind and juice of
    1 large orange

FOR THE TOPPING
225g/8oz/2 cups strawberries,
    quartered
15ml/1 tbsp clear honey

whipped cashew nut cream,
    to serve

Serves 8–10

Variation
This tart is also delicious made with the finely grated rind of 1 lime and the juice of 2 limes, instead of the orange rind and juice.

1 For the base, roughly chop the coconut butter and put it in a small bowl with the coconut oil and sugar over a pan of near-boiling water. Leave for a few minutes, stirring occasionally until the butter and oil have melted.

2 Put the ground almonds, desiccated coconut and raw cacao or cocoa powder in a food processor and blend for a minute or until combined. Drizzle the coconut butter mixture over the dry ingredients then briefly blend again until combined.

3 Tip the mixture into a 23cm/9in loose-bottomed fluted tart tin (pan) and press it evenly over the base and into the fluted sides. Chill while you make the filling.

4 Put the dates in a bowl and pour over enough boiling water to cover them. Leave for 15 minutes. Put the coconut butter and coconut oil in a small bowl and melt as before.

5 Drain the dates and put them in the food processor (no need to wash it first) with about half of the honey. Blend for a minute until fairly smooth, then add the rest of the honey, raw cacao or cocoa powder, orange rind and juice, and the melted coconut butter and oil mixture. Blend until smooth, stopping and scraping down the sides occasionally.

6 Spoon the chocolate mixture into the chilled crust and spread it out evenly with the back of the spoon. Chill in the refrigerator for 2 hours or until firm.

7 Put the strawberries in a bowl and drizzle with the honey. Leave for a few minutes, then stir well.

8 Just before serving remove the chocolate tart from the tart tin and spoon the strawberries on the top. Avoid drizzling the juices over the crust or it will become soggy. Cut the torte into small slices and serve with whipped cashew nut cream.

NUTRITIONAL INFORMATION: Energy 412kcal/1714kJ; Protein 7.1g; Carbohydrate 24.6g, of which sugars 22.8g; Fat 32.5g, of which saturates 20.7g; Cholesterol 0mg; Calcium 65mg; Fibre 6.7g; Sodium 127mg.

TUSCAN RICE CAKE WITH ALMOND MILK

The alcohol from the brandy will evaporate as this bakes in the oven, leaving only the flavour behind. You could use 5ml/1 tsp vanilla extract, if you prefer.

75g/3oz/⅓ cup short grain rice
600ml/1 pint/2½ cups almond milk
sunflower margarine, for greasing
15ml/1 tbsp semolina
4 large eggs
115g/4oz/generous ½ cup caster
   (superfine) sugar
25ml/1½ tbsp brandy
grated rind of ½ unwaxed lemon

Makes 1 cake

Cook's tip
To make a larger rice cake, double the quantity of ingredients and bake the mixture in a 25cm/10in cake tin (pan) for 50 minutes.

NUTRITIONAL INFORMATION:
Energy 1277kcal/5372kJ; Protein 40.2g; Carbohydrate 204.1g, of which sugars 132.7g; Fat 32.5g, of which saturates 7.6g; Cholesterol 924mg; Calcium 187mg; Fibre 0.4g; Sodium 744mg.

1 Put the rice and 350ml/12fl oz/1½ cups of the almond milk into a pan. Boil for 10 minutes, then drain, reserving the almond milk, which will have absorbed some of the starch from the rice. Set aside to cool slightly.

2 Preheat the oven to 180°C/350°F/Gas 4. Grease a deep 20cm/8in fixed-base cake tin (pan) with the margarine, then sprinkle with the semolina. (Do not use a loose-based tin, or all the liquid will leak out.) Turn the cake tin upside down and shake gently to remove any loose semolina.

3 Using an electric whisk, beat the eggs in a large bowl until foaming and pale yellow. Add the sugar gradually, beating constantly, then add the brandy and lemon rind. Stir well.

4 Add the rice and the remaining almond milk (including the reserved milk). Stir well and pour into the cake tin.

5 Bake for 35–40 minutes, or until a cocktail stick (toothpick) inserted into the centre comes out clean. The cake should be well set and golden brown. Serve warm or cold.

COUSCOUS WITH ALMOND MILK AND COCONUT CREAM

Like rice, couscous can be used in desserts as well as savoury dishes. Here it is cooked with almond milk and served with a dried fruit compote flavoured with cinnamon.

300ml/½ pint/1¼ cups water
225g/8oz/1⅓ cups medium
    couscous
50g/2oz/scant ⅓ cup raisins
25g/1oz/2 tbsp sunflower margarine
50g/2oz/¼ cup sugar
120ml/4fl oz/½ cup full-bodied
    almond milk
120ml/4fl oz/½ cup coconut cream

FOR THE FRUIT COMPOTE
225g/8oz/2 cups dried apricots
225g/8oz/1 cup pitted prunes
115/4oz/¾ cup sultanas (golden
    raisins)
115g/4oz/1 cup raw unsalted
    blanched almonds
75g/3oz/¾ cup sugar
1 vanilla pod (bean), split open
1 cinnamon stick

Serves 6

Variations
• The couscous can be served on its own, drizzled with warm clear honey instead of the dried fruit compote, if you prefer.
• The compote is also delicious served chilled on its own with almond milk yogurt.

NUTRITIONAL INFORMATION:
Energy 554kcal/2327kJ; Protein 10.6g; Carbohydrate 83g, of which sugars 63.2g; Fat 22.2g, of which saturates 7.5g; Cholesterol 0mg; Calcium 123mg; Fibre 7.6g; Sodium 80mg.

1 Prepare the fruit compote a couple of days in advance. Put the dried fruit and the almonds in a bowl and pour in just enough water to cover. Gently stir in the sugar and add the vanilla pod and cinnamon stick. Cover and leave the fruit and nuts to soak for 48 hours, during which time the water and sugar will form a lovely golden-coloured syrup.

2 To make the couscous, bring the water to the boil in a large pan. Stir in the couscous and raisins, and cook gently over a medium heat for 1–2 minutes, until the water has been absorbed. Remove the pan from the heat, cover it tightly and leave the couscous to steam for 10–15 minutes. Meanwhile, poach the compote over a gentle heat, until warmed through.

3 Tip the couscous into a bowl and separate the grains with your fingertips. Melt the margarine and pour it over the couscous. Sprinkle the sugar over the top then, using your fingertips, rub the margarine and sugar into the couscous. Divide the mixture among six bowls.

4 Heat the almond milk and coconut cream together in a small pan until it is just about to boil. Pour over the couscous and serve immediately with the dried fruit compote.

BREAD, APPLE AND ALMOND MILK PUDDING

Based on breadcrumbs, dried apples and raisins, this simple, nutritious dessert has a set custard-like texture and can be quickly made from standby ingredients. Serve with a spoonful of home-made apricot conserve or a good-quality bought one.

50g/2oz/¼ cup sunflower
   margarine, melted, plus extra
   for greasing
200g/7oz white bread slices,
   crusts removed
150ml/¼ pint/⅔ cup almond milk
4 eggs, separated
45ml/3 tbsp caster (superfine)
   sugar
200g/7oz sliced dried apples,
   roughly chopped
50g/2oz/scant ½ cup raisins
75g/2oz/¼ cup flaked (sliced)
   almonds

Serves 4–6

Variation
Try other dried fruit and nut combinations in this dessert, such as dried peaches and walnut milk, or dried pears and hazelnut milk.

Cook's tip
Choose a white bread, preferably made with unbleached flour for this dessert; wholemeal (wholewheat) bread will make it stodgy and heavy.

NUTRITIONAL INFORMATION:
Energy 412kcal/1731kJ; Protein 11.4g; Carbohydrate 51.1g, of which sugars 35.1g; Fat 19.5g, of which saturates 3.4g; Cholesterol 154mg; Calcium 101mg; Fibre 5.3g; Sodium 315mg.

1 Preheat the oven to 180°C/350°F/Gas 4 and generously grease a 15 x 20cm/6 x 8in ovenproof dish with margarine.

2 Process the bread in a food processor or blender until you have breadcrumbs. Transfer these to a bowl and add the almond milk and melted margarine, mixing well.

3 In another bowl, whisk the egg yolks and sugar until light and creamy. Fold the apples and raisins into the whisked egg and sugar mixture. Add this to the breadcrumb mixture, and combine well.

4 Put the egg whites into a clean, grease-free bowl and whisk until they form stiff peaks. Stir a spoonful of the whites into the breadcrumb mixture to lighten it, then fold in the remaining whites. Pour into the prepared dish.

5 Sprinkle with the almonds and bake for 25–30 minutes, or until golden and firm.

WINTER FRUIT CRUMBLE WITH ALMOND BUTTER

This almond butter crumble uses pears and dried fruit in its base, making it ideal for the winter months. At other times of the year, try gooseberries with a dash of elderflower cordial, rhubarb flavoured with ginger, or apples and blackberries.

30ml/2 tbsp almond butter
150g/5oz/10 tbsp hard baking
    margarine
175g/6oz/1½ cups plain
    (all-purpose) flour
50g/2oz/½ cup dried almond flour
    or ground almonds
115g/4oz/½ cup light muscovado
    (brown) sugar
40g/1½oz flaked (sliced) almonds
1 unwaxed orange
16 ready-to-eat dried apricots
4 firm ripe pears

Serves 6

Cook's tip
Serve this crumble with almond milk custard (see page 107, using almond milk instead of walnut milk).

NUTRITIONAL INFORMATION:
Energy 627kcal/2632kJ; Protein 9.3g; Carbohydrate 88.4g, of which sugars 58.2g; Fat 28.6g, of which saturates 5g; Cholesterol 1mg; Calcium 131mg; Fibre 11.6g; Sodium 187mg.

1 Put the almond butter and margarine in a bowl and blend together. Scoop up on to a piece of baking parchment so that it fits in the refrigerator or freezer, and chill for 30 minutes (or freeze for 10 minutes), until hardened.

2 Preheat the oven to 190°C/375°F/Gas 5. Sift the flour into a bowl, stir in the almond flour or ground almonds, then add the almond margarine and rub into the flour until the mixture resembles rough breadcrumbs. Stir in 75g/3oz/⅓ cup sugar and the flaked almonds.

3 Finely grate 5ml/1 tsp rind from the orange and squeeze out its juice. Halve the apricots and put them in a shallow ovenproof dish. Peel the pears, remove their cores and cut the fruit into small pieces. Arrange the pears over the apricots.

4 Stir the orange rind into the orange juice and sprinkle over the fruit. Sprinkle the remaining brown sugar over the top. Cover the fruit with the crumble mixture and smooth over. Bake for about 40 minutes, until the topping is golden brown and the fruit is soft (test it with the point of a sharp knife).

SEEDED NUTTY SPELT BREAD WITH SUNFLOWER MILK

A mixture of quinoa and spelt flour is used to make this rustic loaf. Spelt is an ancient grain (dating back more than 5,000 years), and has a lower gluten content than wheat flour. The seeds and sunflower milk provide slow-release carbohydrates.

225g/8oz/2 cups quinoa flour
225g/8oz/2 cups spelt flour
10ml/2 tsp easy-blend (rapid-rise)
   dried yeast
10ml/2 tsp salt
60ml/4 tbsp sugar
25g/1oz/¼ cup mixed seeds
   (sunflower, pumpkin, flax and
   poppy seeds), plus 15ml/1 tbsp
   extra, for sprinkling
25g/1oz/¼ cup chopped raw
   unsalted nuts, such as walnuts
   or hazelnuts
250ml/8fl oz/1 cup sunflower seed
   milk, plus extra to glaze
50ml/2fl oz/¼ cup boiling water
oil, for greasing

Serves 8

Cook's tip
You can use a breadmaker to make this loaf, using a basic wholegrain programme. Add the nuts and seeds to the dough halfway through the cycle, or follow the manufacturer's instructions.

1 Sift the flours into a large bowl, add the dried yeast, salt, sugar, mixed seeds and chopped nuts, and stir to combine. Make a well in the centre.

2 Mix the sunflower seed milk and boiling water together in a bowl and pour into the well. Stir, mixing in the flour gradually, to form a pliable dough. Transfer the dough to a floured board, and knead by hand for 6–8 minutes, or in an electric mixer with a dough hook for 4–5 minutes, until soft and elastic.

3 To knead by hand, hold the dough with one hand and stretch it with the palm of the other hand, then fold it back. Turn the dough 90 degrees and repeat this process for the required time.

4 Place the dough in a clean bowl, cover it with a damp cloth and leave it in a warm place for 1–1½ hours, until the dough has nearly doubled in size.

5 Knock back (punch down) the dough and knead it for a couple of minutes. Cover it with the damp cloth again and set it aside to prove for another 30 minutes, until doubled in size. Preheat the oven to 220°C/425°F/Gas 7.

6 Oil a 450g/1lb loaf tin (pan), or a baking sheet. Shape the dough to neatly fill the tin or, if using the baking sheet, split it into three strands and plait (braid) it for a more decorative loaf.

7 With a sharp knife, score the top of the loaf lengthways and across, to help the dough rise. Brush the top with milk and sprinkle with seeds.

8 Bake for 35–40 minutes, until the loaf is risen and golden, and sounds hollow on the base when tapped (you will have to remove it from the tin to test this). Remove from the tin or baking sheet, and cool on a wire rack for at least 20 minutes.

NUTRITIONAL INFORMATION: Energy 300kcal/1254kJ; Protein 5.8g; Carbohydrate 54.4g, of which sugars 8.1g; Fat 6.1g, of which saturates 0.6g; Cholesterol 0mg; Calcium 23mg; Fibre 2.4g; Sodium 496mg.

BROWN SCONES WITH OAT MILK

These unusually light scones are virtually fat-free, so they must be eaten very fresh – warm from the oven if possible, but definitely on the day of baking.

vegetable oil, for greasing
115g/4oz/1 cup self-raising (self-
   rising) flour, plus extra for dusting
115g/4oz/1 cup wholemeal
   (whole-wheat) self-raising
   (self-rising) flour
5ml/1 tsp baking powder
1.5ml/¼ tsp salt
about 350ml/12fl oz/1½ cups oat
   milk, plus extra for glazing

Makes about 8

Cook's tip
These savoury scones are delicious served with soup, or you can spread them with a little coconut butter or sunflower spread and top with a spoonful of fruity jam.

NUTRITIONAL INFORMATION:
Energy 117kcal/497kJ; Protein 3.2g;
Carbohydrate 20.7g, of which
sugars 2.6g; Fat 1g, of which
saturates 0.1g; Cholesterol 0mg;
Calcium 63mg; Fibre 2.3g; Sodium
126mg.

1 Preheat the oven to 220°C/425°F/Gas 7. Grease a baking sheet with oil and dust with flour.

2 Sift the flours, baking powder and salt into a bowl, adding the bran left in the sieve (strainer). Make a well in the centre, pour in almost all the oat milk and mix, adding milk as needed to make a soft, moist dough. Do not overmix.

3 Lightly dust a surface with flour, turn out the dough and dust it with flour.

4 Press out the dough to a thickness of 4cm/1½in. Cut out eight scones with a 5cm/2in fluted pastry (cookie) cutter. Place on the baking sheet and brush the tops with oat milk or leave unglazed and dust with a little flour.

5 Bake the scones for about 12 minutes, until well risen and golden brown. Remove to a cooling rack and enjoy warm.

FRUIT MALT LOAF WITH HEMP SEED MILK

Malt extract gives this fruity loaf its chewy consistency and hemp seed milk adds depth of flavour. Cut in slices and spread with coconut butter or sunflower spread.

vegetable oil, for greasing
250g/9oz/2¼ cups wholemeal
  (whole-wheat) self-raising
  (self-rising) flour
pinch of salt
2.5ml/½ tsp bicarbonate of soda
  (baking soda)
175g/6oz/1 cup mixed dried fruit
15ml/1 tbsp malt extract
250ml/8fl oz/1 cup hemp seed milk
coconut butter or sunflower
  spread, to serve

Serves 8–10

Variation
For a tropical fruit loaf, use chopped dried pineapple and dried mango and Brazil nut milk instead of the dried mixed fruit and hemp seed milk. Add 5ml/1 tsp ground ginger to the dry ingredients.

Cook's tip
Wrap the cooled loaf in baking parchment, then in foil. It will keep for up to 3 weeks. The flavour and texture of the loaf improves after a few days' keeping.

NUTRITIONAL INFORMATION:
Energy 155kcal/659kJ; Protein 4.8g; Carbohydrate 30.6g, of which sugars 14.9g; Fat 2.4g, of which saturates 0.3g; Cholesterol 0mg; Calcium 28mg; Fibre 3.9g; Sodium 82mg.

1 Preheat the oven to 160°C/325°F/Gas 3. Grease and line a 900g/2lb loaf tin (pan) with baking parchment. Put the dry ingredients in a large bowl.

2 Heat the malt extract and hemp seed milk in a pan, stirring until blended. Alternatively, heat the hemp seed milk and malt extract in the microwave for 1 minute, stir and then heat for a further 30 seconds, or until the malt extract has blended into the hemp seed milk. Mix into the dry ingredients.

3 Spoon into the prepared tin. Bake for 45 minutes, or until a skewer inserted into the loaf comes out clean.

4 Leave to stand for 5 minutes, then turn out on to a wire rack to go cold. Remove the lining paper.

PEANUT BUTTER TEABREAD

This peanut-milk enriched loaf also contains crunchy peanut butter, which adds protein and other nutrients. Serve sliced, lightly toasted and spread with honey or jam.

225g/8oz/2 cups plain
   (all-purpose) flour
7.5ml/1½ tsp baking powder
2.5ml/½ tsp bicarbonate of soda
   (baking soda)
50g/2oz/¼ cup hard baking
   margarine, plus extra
   for greasing
175g/6oz/½ cup crunchy
   peanut butter
50g/2oz/generous ¼ cup caster
   (superfine) sugar
2 eggs, beaten
250ml/8fl oz/1 cup peanut milk
25g/1oz/¼ cup roasted salted
   peanuts

Serves 10

Variation
For cinnamon raisin peanut butter teabread, add 10ml/ 2 tsp ground cinnamon when sifting the flour and stir in 150g/5oz/1 cup raisins when you are adding the dry ingredients.

NUTRITIONAL INFORMATION:
Energy 288kcal/1202kJ; Protein 8.5g; Carbohydrate 27.3g, of which sugars 7.7g; Fat 16.7g, of which saturates 3.7g; Cholesterol 46mg; Calcium 59mg; Fibre 0.9g; Sodium 231mg.

1 Preheat the oven to 180°C/350°F/Gas 4. Grease and line a 900g/2lb loaf tin (pan) with baking parchment.

2 Sift together the flour, baking powder and bicarbonate of soda into a large bowl.

3 Put the margarine and peanut butter in a large bowl and beat together with a wooden spoon to soften, then beat in the sugar until very light and fluffy.

4 Gradually whisk in the eggs a little at a time, then beat in the peanut milk with the sifted flour and mix until incorporated. Pour into the prepared tin and sprinkle the peanuts on top.

5 Bake for 1 hour or until a skewer inserted into the centre comes out clean. Cool in the tin for 5 minutes, then turn out on to a wire rack. Remove the lining paper.

COCONUT, ALMOND AND RASPBERRY-FILLED ROLL

This light and airy whisked sponge cake is flavoured with almonds and rolled up with a filling of fresh raspberries and whipped coconut cream.

vegetable oil, for greasing
4 eggs
115g/4oz/generous ½ cup caster
   (superfine) sugar, plus 15ml/
   1 tbsp for dusting
150g/5oz/1¼ cups plain
   (all-purpose) flour, sifted
25g/1oz/¼ cup dried almond flour
   or ground almonds
15ml/1 tbsp desiccated (dry
   unsweetened shredded) coconut

FOR THE FILLING
275g/10oz/1⅔ cups raspberries
250ml/8fl oz/1 cup whipped
   coconut cream
toasted flaked (sliced) almonds,
   to decorate

Serves 8

NUTRITIONAL INFORMATION:
Energy 306kcal/1283kJ; Protein
7.7g; Carbohydrate 35.6g, of
which sugars 18.9g; Fat 15.8g, of
which saturates 11.4g; Cholesterol
116mg; Calcium 64mg; Fibre 2.4g;
Sodium 46mg.

1 Preheat the oven to 200°C/400°F/Gas 6. Grease and line a 33 × 23cm/13 × 9in Swiss roll tin (jelly roll pan) with baking parchment.

2 Put the eggs and sugar in a large bowl and beat with an electric whisk for about 10 minutes, or until the mixture is thick and pale. Sift the flour over the mixture and gently fold in with the almond flour or ground almonds, using a metal spoon.

3 Spoon the batter into the tin and smooth level. Bake for 10–12 minutes, or until the sponge is well risen and springy to the touch.

4 Dust a sheet of baking parchment with the desiccated coconut and sugar. Turn out the cake on to the paper, and leave it to cool with the tin in place. Lift the tin off the cooled cake and peel away the lining paper.

5 To make the filling, fold 250g/8oz/1¼ cups of the raspberries into the whipped coconut cream, and spread over the cake, leaving a border. Carefully roll up the cake from a narrow end, using the paper to lift the sponge. Serve decorated with the remaining raspberries and the toasted flaked almonds.

PINEAPPLE UPSIDE-DOWN CAKE WITH BRAZIL NUT MILK

This light and moist cake has a sticky ginger glaze over stem ginger and pineapple pieces, which are arranged in the cake tin before the cake batter is added.

20g/¾oz/1½ tbsp coconut oil or sunflower margarine, plus extra for greasing
2 pieces preserved stem ginger, chopped, plus 60ml/4 tbsp syrup
450g/1lb can pineapple pieces in natural juice, drained
250g/9oz/2¼ cups wholemeal (whole-wheat) self-raising (self-rising) flour
15ml/1 tbsp baking powder
5ml/1 tsp ground ginger
5ml/1 tsp ground cinnamon
115g/4oz/½ cup soft light brown sugar
250ml/8fl oz/1 cup Brazil nut milk or coconut milk
1 banana, peeled

Serves 8

NUTRITIONAL INFORMATION:
Energy 204kcal/866kJ; Protein 4.1g; Carbohydrate 43.3g, of which sugars 25.5g; Fat 2.9g, of which saturates 0.6g; Cholesterol 0mg; Calcium 50mg; Fibre 3.9g; Sodium 113mg.

1 Preheat the oven to 180°C/235°F/Gas 4. Grease and line a 20cm/8in round deep cake tin (pan).

2 Melt the coconut oil or sunflower margarine in a small pan with the ginger syrup. Turn up the heat and cook until the liquid thickens. Pour into the tin and smooth out to the sides.

3 Arrange the stem ginger and one-third of the pineapple pieces in the syrup in the tin. Set aside.

4 Sift together the flour, baking powder and spices into a large bowl, then stir in the sugar.

5 Blend together the Brazil nut or coconut milk, the remaining pineapple and the banana until almost smooth, then add to the flour. Stir until thoroughly combined. Spoon the mixture over the pineapple and ginger pieces in the tin and smooth level.

6 Bake for 45 minutes, or until a skewer inserted into the centre comes out clean. Leave to cool slightly, then place a serving plate over the tin and turn upside down. Remove the lining paper.

ALMOND CAKE

Toasted almonds and almond butter are the main ingredients in this cake, giving it a nutty flavour. Serve it warm with some almond milk yogurt or almond ice cream.

175g/6oz/1½ cups raw unsalted blanched almonds, plus extra for decorating
75g/3oz/¾ cup icing (confectioners') sugar, plus extra for dusting
3 eggs
25g/1oz/2 tbsp coconut oil or sunflower margarine, plus extra for greasing
30ml/2 tbsp smooth almond butter
2.5ml/½ tsp almond extract
15g/½oz/2 tbsp plain (all-purpose) flour
15g/½oz/2 tbsp dried almond flour or extra plain flour
3 egg whites
15ml/1 tbsp caster (superfine) sugar
almond milk yogurt or almond milk ice cream, to serve

Serves 4–6

Variation
For a chocolate hazelnut cake, use hazelnuts instead of the almonds and chocolate hazelnut spread instead of the almond butter. Substitute 15ml/1 tbsp of the flour with raw cacao or (unsweetened) cocoa powder.

NUTRITIONAL INFORMATION:
Energy 373kcal/1554kJ; Protein 13.1g; Carbohydrate 22.7g, of which sugars 17g; Fat 26.4g, of which saturates 3.3g; Cholesterol 116mg; Calcium 99mg; Fibre 1.2g; Sodium 106mg.

1 Preheat the oven to 160°C/325°F/Gas 3. Grease and line a 23cm/9in round shallow cake tin (pan) with baking parchment.

2 Spread the almonds on a baking sheet and bake for 10 minutes. Allow to cool. Roughly chop, then grind them with half of the icing sugar in a food processor. Transfer to a large bowl.

3 Increase the oven temperature to 200°C/400°F/Gas 6. Add the whole eggs and the remaining icing sugar to the bowl. With an electric whisk, beat until the mixture forms a trail when the beaters are lifted away.

4 In a small pan, melt the coconut oil or sunflower margarine. Add the almond butter and stir until blended, then mix into the nut and egg mixture with the almond extract. Sift over the flour and fold in with the almond flour or extra plain flour.

5 Whisk the egg whites until they form soft peaks. Add the sugar. Beat until stiff. Fold into the batter. Spoon into the cake tin.

6 Bake for 15–20 minutes, until golden. Turn out and remove the paper. Decorate with the extra almonds and dust with icing sugar.

CASHEW NUT BUTTER COOKIES

These crumbly cookies are quick and easy to make and contain just a few ingredients.
If you enjoy sneaking a spoonful of nut butter from the jar, you will love these!

225g/8oz/1 cup smooth cashew
   nut butter
30ml/2 tbsp maple syrup
10ml/2 tsp raw cacao or
   (unsweetened) cocoa powder
2.5ml/½ tsp icing (confectioners')
   sugar

Makes 12

Variation
For thumbprint cookies, use
your thumb, fingertip or, for
a neat round hole, the end
of a wooden spoon dipped in
icing (confectioners') sugar to
make a hole in the middle of
each cookie, before baking.
After baking and while the
cookies are still hot, spoon
or pipe a little smooth jam or
some chocolate hazelnut
spread into the hole and
leave to cool.

NUTRITIONAL INFORMATION:
Energy 119kcal/499kJ; Protein 3.7g;
Carbohydrate 6.8g, of which sugars
1.5g; Fat 9.6g, of which saturates
2.5g; Cholesterol 0mg; Calcium
3mg; Fibre 0.1g; Sodium 8mg.

1 Preheat the oven to 180°C/350°F/Gas 4. Line a baking sheet
with baking parchment.

2 Put 115g/4oz/½ cup of the cashew nut butter and 15ml/1 tbsp
of the maple syrup into a bowl and combine with a spoon.

3 Put the remaining cashew nut butter and maple syrup in a
bowl. Sift over 7.5ml/1½ tsp of the raw cacao or cocoa powder.
Mix together until blended.

4 Shape each batch of mixture into six walnut-sized balls.
Flatten these slightly, then arrange on the baking sheet, spacing
them slightly apart to allow room for the cookies to spread.

5 Bake the cookies for 5–7 minutes, or until beginning to
brown around the edges. Remove from the oven and dust the
plain ones with icing sugar and the chocolate ones with the
remaining 2.5ml/½ tsp cacao or cocoa powder. Leave to cool on
the baking sheet. Store in an airtight container for up to 4 days.

PEANUT BUTTER COOKIES

There are many versions of this well-known cookie. These are rolled in peanuts for a crunchier texture. If liked, you can pair them together with jam.

115g/4oz/½ cup hard baking margarine, softened
115g/4oz/½ cup light muscovado (brown) sugar
115g/4oz/½ cup smooth peanut butter
1 egg, lightly beaten
150g/5oz/1¼ cups self-raising (self-rising) flour
2.5ml/½ tsp baking powder
175g/6oz/1½ cups raw unsalted skinned peanuts, chopped

Makes 12

1 Preheat the oven to 180°C/350°F/Gas 4. Line two baking sheets with baking parchment.

2 Put the margarine and sugar into a bowl and beat together until creamy. Add the peanut butter and beat until combined.

3 Add the egg a little at a time, beating well after each addition. Sift the flour and baking powder over the mixture and stir everything together.

4 Put the chopped peanuts on a plate. Scoop up heaped teaspoons of the mixture and roll into balls (the mixture will be quite sticky, so chill it first for a few minutes, if necessary).

5 Roll the balls in the chopped nuts, then place them on the baking sheets, spacing them well apart, and flatten slightly.

6 Bake the cookies for 8–10 minutes or until the nuts are lightly browned. Leave on the baking sheets for 5 minutes to firm up, then transfer them to a wire rack. Store in an airtight container for up to 5 days.

NUTRITIONAL INFORMATION:
Energy 299kcal/1246kJ; Protein 7.7g; Carbohydrate 22.6g, of which sugars 11.7g; Fat 20.3g, of which saturates 4.3g; Cholesterol 19mg; Calcium 64mg; Fibre 0.5g; Sodium 176mg.

INDEX

açai berries 35
agave syrup 36
almond butter 6, 43
Almond Cake 123
Apricot and Almond Butter Stuffed Chicken 97
Chicken Fricassée with Almond Butter 96
Lamb in Rose-scented Almond Sauce 102
Onion Soup with Almond Butter and Milk 68
Pork Steak with Almond Stuffing 100
Winter Fruit Crumble with Almond Butter 115
Almond Chutney 43
almond cream: Garganelli with Almond Cream Ragù 88
Almond Milk 6, 24–5
Almond Milk and Blackberry Muffins 58
Almond Milk and Pistachio Milk Ice Creams 105
Almond Milk and Rose Water Blancmange 106
Almond Milk Morning Rolls 57
Almond Milk Pudding 109
Bean Chilli with Almond Milk Cornbread Topping 90
Bread, Apple and Almond Milk Pudding 114
Chilled Almond Milk and Garlic Soup 64
Couscous with Almond Milk and Coconut Cream 113
Fish in Creamy Almond Sauce 92
Kedgeree with Almond Milk 61
Lamb in Rose-scented Almond Sauce 102
Light Almond Milk 25
Mushroom, Courgette and Almond Milk Lasagne 86
Onion Soup with Almond Butter and Milk 68
Simple Unsweetened Almond Milk 24
Tuscan Rice Cake with Almond Milk 112
Almond Milk Cheese 38
Almond Milk Yogurt: Almond Yogurt with Pomegranate and Grapefruit 54
Aubergine Dip with Tahini and Almond Yogurt 72
Lamb in Rose-scented Almond Sauce 102
Papaya and Almond Yogurt Lassi 63
almonds 10
Almond Cake 123
Almond Milk and Blackberry Muffins 58
Almond Milk Pudding 109
blanching 24
Chocolate, Coconut and Almond Torte 110
Coconut, Seed and Nut Granola with Nut Yogurt 55
apples: Apple and Walnut Milk Flummery 107
Bread, Apple and Almond Milk Pudding 114
Carrot, Apple and Cashew Nut Milk Soup 69
Gado-gado 80
apricots: Apricot and Almond Butter Stuffed Chicken 97

Couscous with Almond Milk and Coconut Cream 113
Fruit and Seed Butter Breakfast Bars 59
Winter Fruit Crumble with Almond Butter 115
aubergines (eggplants): Aubergine Dip with Tahini and Almond Yogurt 72
Roasted Vegetables with Peanut Sauce 85

baking 116–25
bananas: Banana, Pineapple and Brazil Nut Milk Shake 62
Oat and Pecan Nut Milk Pancakes with Bananas 56
beans: Bean Chilli with Almond Milk Cornbread Topping 90
beansprouts: Sichuan Noodles with Sesame Sauce 89
beef: Thai Beef Curry in Sweet Peanut Sauce 101
blackberries: Almond Milk and Blackberry Muffins 58
blancmange 7
Almond Milk and Rose Water Blancmange 106
blending milks 34
Brazil Nut Milk 28
Banana, Pineapple and Brazil Nut Milk Shake 62
Pineapple Upside-down Cake with Brazil Nut Milk 122
Brazil nuts 10–11
bread: Bread, Apple and Almond Milk Pudding 114
Chestnut Mushrooms on Toast 60
Pumpkin, Chicken and Pumpkin Seed Milk Soup 71
Seafood and Cashew Nut Milk Purée 75
Seeded Nutty Spelt Bread with Sunflower Milk 116
Breakfast Bars, Fruit and Seed Butter 59
breakfasts 54–61

cacao 34
Baked Coffee Custards with Macadamia Nut Cream 108
cakes: Almond Cake 123
Coconut, Almond and Raspberry-filled Roll 121
Pineapple Upside-down Cake with Brazil Nut Milk 122
Carrot, Apple and Cashew Nut Milk Soup 69
Cashew Nut Butter 6, 44
Cashew Nut Butter Cookies 124
Prawns in a Poppy Seed and Cashew Nut Sauce 93
Cashew Nut Cream 50
Haddock and Salmon Terrine with Cashew Cream 76
Sprout Salad with Cashew Nut Cream Dressing 82
Cashew Nut Milk 20–1
Carrot, Apple and Cashew Nut Milk Soup 69
Curried Cauliflower and Cashew Nut Milk Soup 64
Haddock and Salmon Terrine with Cashew Cream 76
Indian-style Cashew Nut Milk and Mango Drink 63

Seafood and Cashew Nut Milk Purée 75
Simple Cashew Nut Milk 20–1
Smoked Cod Omelette with Cashew Nut Milk 60
cashew nut yogurt: Turkey in a Coconut and Cashew Nut Sauce 95
cashew nuts 11
Chicken Salad with Nuts and Coconut Cream 83
Seafood and Cashew Nut Milk Purée 75
Turkey in a Coconut and Cashew Nut Sauce 95
cauliflower: Curried Cauliflower and Cashew Nut Milk Soup 64
Chestnut Butter 47
Chestnut Milk 29
Chestnut Mushrooms on Toast 60
chestnuts 12
peeling 29
chia seeds 35
chicken: Apricot and Almond Butter Stuffed Chicken 97
Chicken Fricassée with Almond Butter 96
Chicken, Pork and Potatoes in Peanut Sauce 98
Chicken Salad with Nuts and Coconut Cream 83
Chicken Satay 79
Garganelli with Almond Cream Ragù 88
Pumpkin, Chicken and Pumpkin Seed Milk Soup 71
chickpeas: Tahini Hummus 74
chocolate 34
Chocolate, Coconut and Almond Torte 110
Chocolate Hazelnut Spread 46
Chutney, Almond 43
coconut: Chocolate, Coconut and Almond Torte 110
Coconut, Almond and Raspberry-filled Roll 121
Fruit and Seed Butter Breakfast Bars 59
Coconut Butter 47
Chocolate, Coconut and Almond Torte 110
Coconut, Seed and Nut Granola with Nut Yogurt 55
Coconut Cream 32
Chicken Salad with Nuts and Coconut Cream 83
Coconut, Almond and Raspberry-filled Roll 121
Couscous with Almond Milk and Coconut Cream 113
coconut flour 39
coconut milk 6, 32
Coconut Milk Ice Cream 104
Gado-gado 80
Pork and Pineapple Coconut Milk Curry 99
Porridge with Coconut Milk and Dates 54
Pumpkin, Peanut and Coconut Milk Curry 84
Seafood and Cashew Nut Milk Purée 75
Seafood Chowder with Coconut Milk 70
Thai Beef Curry in Sweet Peanut Sauce 101

Turkey in a Coconut and Cashew Nut Sauce 95
coconut palm sugar/syrup 36
coconuts 12
preparing a mature coconut 33
coffee: Baked Coffee Custards with Macadamia Nut Cream 108
cookies: Cashew Nut Butter Cookies 124
Peanut Butter Cookies 125
cornmeal: Bean Chilli with Almond Milk Cornbread Topping 90
courgettes (zucchini): Mushroom, Courgette and Almond Milk Lasagne 86
Roasted Vegetables with Peanut Sauce 85
Couscous with Almond Milk and Coconut Cream 113
Cranachan, Raspberry and Hazelnut Yogurt 55
Creamed Coconut 32–3
Whipped Coconut Cream 33
curries: Curried Cauliflower and Cashew Nut Milk Soup 64
Pork and Pineapple Coconut Milk Curry 99
Pumpkin, Peanut and Coconut Milk Curry 84

dairy milk 6
dates 36
Banana, Pineapple and Brazil Nut Milk Shake 62
Chocolate, Coconut and Almond Torte 110
Porridge with Coconut Milk and Dates 54
desserts 104–115
diabetes 9
dips: Aubergine Dip with Tahini and Almond Yogurt 72
Spicy Walnut Yogurt Dip 73
dried fruits 35
Fruit Malt Loaf with Hemp Seed Milk 119
drinks 62–3

eggs: Baked Coffee Custards with Macadamia Nut Cream 108
Gado-gado 80
Kedgeree with Almond Milk 61
Smoked Cod Omelette with Cashew Nut Milk 60
equipment, tools and 18–19

fish: Fish in Creamy Almond Sauce 92
Kedgeree with Almond Milk 61
Seafood and Cashew Nut Milk Purée 75
Seafood Chowder with Coconut Milk 70
Smoked Cod Omelette with Cashew Nut Milk 60
flavouring milks 34–5
Flummery, Apple and Walnut Milk 107
fruit juices, fresh 35

Gado-gado 80
Garganelli with Almond Cream Ragù 88
garlic: Chilled Almond Milk and Garlic Soup 64
ginger: Pear, Ginger and Walnut Milk Shake 62

goji berries 35
granola: Coconut, Seed and Nut
    Granola with Nut Yogurt 55
grapefruit: Almond Yogurt with
    Pomegranate and Grapefruit 54

Hazelnut Butter 6, 45
    Parsnip Soup with Hazelnut Butter
    and Milk 66
Hazelnut Milk 6, 26
    Leek and Hazelnut Milk Tart 91
    Parsnip Soup with Hazelnut Butter
    and Milk 66
hazelnut yogurt: Raspberry and
    Hazelnut Yogurt Cranachan 55
hazelnuts 12–13
    Chocolate Hazelnut Spread 46
    Coconut, Seed and Nut Granola
    with Nut Yogurt 55
    roasting and skinning 26
heart health 9
Hemp Seed Milk 31
    Fresh Mushroom Soup with Hemp
    Seed Milk 67
    Fruit Malt Loaf with Hemp Seed
    Milk 119
hemp seeds 17
history of nut and seed milks and
    butters 6–7
honey 36–7
    Coconut, Seed and Nut Granola
    with Nut Yogurt 55
Hummus, Tahini 74

ice cream: Almond Milk and Pistachio
    Milk Ice Creams 105
    Coconut Milk Ice Cream 104

Kedgeree with Almond Milk 61

Lamb in Rose-scented Almond Sauce
    102
Lasagne, Mushroom, Courgette and
    Almond Milk 86
Lassi, Papaya and Almond Yogurt 63
lecithin 23
leeks: Leek and Hazelnut Milk Tart 91
    Leek, Oatmeal and Oat Milk Broth
    65
    Roasted Vegetables with Peanut
    Sauce 85

Macadamia Nut Butter 45
Macadamia Nut Milk 27
    Baked Coffee Custards with
    Macadamia Nut Cream 108
macadamia nuts 13
main courses 84–103
mangoes: Indian-style Cashew Nut
    Milk and Mango Drink 63
Muffins, Almond Milk and Blackberry
    58
mushrooms: Chestnut Mushrooms on
    Toast 60
    Fresh Mushroom Soup with Hemp
    Seed Milk 67
    Mushroom, Courgette and Almond
    Milk Lasagne 86
    Pumpkin, Peanut and Coconut Milk
    Curry 84
mussels: Seafood Chowder with
    Coconut Milk 70

noodles: Gado-gado 80
    Sichuan Noodles with Sesame
    Sauce 89
nut butters, ways to use 50
Nut Creams
    Cashew Nut Cream 50

Simple Nut Cream 50
Nut Flour 38–9
Nut Milk Yogurt 37
nut milks 20–9
    almond milk 24–5
    milks of different strengths 23
    other nut milks 26–9
    soaking nuts 22
    storage and shelf life 22
    thickening and emulsifying 23
nuts: buying and storing 17
    definition 15
    for different lifestyles 8
    soaking 22

Oat Milk 31
    Brown Scones with Oat Milk 118
    Leek, Oatmeal and Oat Milk Broth
    65
oatmeal: Leek, Oatmeal and Oat Milk
    Broth 65
oats: Coconut, Seed and Nut Granola
    with Nut Yogurt 55
    Fruit and Seed Butter Breakfast
    Bars 59
    Oat and Pecan Nut Milk Pancakes
    with Bananas 56
    Porridge with Coconut Milk and
    Dates 54
    Raspberry and Hazelnut Yogurt
    Cranachan 55
omega-3 fatty acids 9
Omelette with Cashew Nut Milk,
    Smoked Cod 60
Onion Soup with Almond Butter and
    Milk 68

paleolithic diet 8
pancakes: Oat and Pecan Nut Milk
    Pancakes with Bananas 56
Papaya and Almond Yogurt Lassi 63
Parsnip Soup with Hazelnut Butter
    and Milk 66
Peanut Butter 6
    Crunchy Peanut Butter 42
    Chicken Satay 79
    Gado-gado 80
    Peanut Butter and Tofu Cutlets 78
    Peanut Butter Teabread 120
    Roasted Vegetables with Peanut
    Butter 85
    Thai Beef Curry in Sweet Peanut
    Sauce 101
    history of 7
    Smooth Peanut Butter 40–1
    Chicken, Pork and Potatoes in
    Peanut Sauce 98
    Peanut Butter Cookies 125
peanuts 13
    Gado-gado 80
    Peanut Butter Cookies 125
    Pumpkin, Peanut and Coconut Milk
    Curry 84
    Roasted Vegetables with Peanut
    Sauce 85
    Seafood and Cashew Nut Milk
    Purée 75
    skinning and roasting 41
pears: Gado-gado 80
    Pear, Ginger and Walnut Milk
    Shake 62
    Winter Fruit Crumble with Almond
    Butter 115
Pecan Nut Milk 27
    Oat and Pecan Nut Milk Pancakes
    with Bananas 56
pecan nuts 14
Pesto, Dairy-free Pine Nut 51
pine nut butter 50

pine nuts 14
    Dairy-free Pine Nut Pesto 51
pineapples: Banana, Pineapple and
    Brazil Nut Milk Shake 62
    Gado-gado 80
    Pineapple Upside-down Cake with
    Brazil Nut Milk 122
    Pork and Pineapple Coconut Milk
    Curry 99
Pistachio Milk 28
    Almond Milk and Pistachio Milk Ice
    Creams 105
Pistachio Nut Butter 45
pistachio nuts 15
    Almond Milk Pudding 109
pomegranates: Almond Yogurt with
    Pomegranate and Grapefruit 54
poppy seeds: Prawns in a Poppy Seed
    and Cashew Nut Sauce 93
pork: Chicken, Pork and Potatoes in
    Peanut Sauce 98
    Pork Steak with Almond Stuffing 100
    Porridge with Coconut Milk and
    Dates 54
potatoes: Chicken, Pork and Potatoes
    in Peanut Sauce 98
    Seafood Chowder with Coconut
    Milk 70
prawns (shrimp): Prawns in a Poppy
    Seed and Cashew Nut Sauce 93
    Seafood and Cashew Nut Milk
    Purée 75
    Seafood Chowder with Coconut
    Milk 70
prunes: Couscous with Almond Milk
    and Coconut Cream 113
pumpkin: Pumpkin, Chicken and
    Pumpkin Seed Milk Soup 71
    Pumpkin, Peanut and Coconut Milk
    Curry 84
Pumpkin Seed Butter 5, 48
    Fruit and Seed Butter Breakfast
    Bars 59
Pumpkin Seed Milk 30
    Pumpkin, Chicken and Pumpkin
    Seed Milk Soup 71
pumpkin seeds 17

quinoa flour: Seeded Nutty Spelt
    Bread with Sunflower Milk 116

raisins: Coconut, Seed and Nut
    Granola with Nut Yogurt 55
    Fruit and Seed Butter Breakfast
    Bars 59
raspberries: Coconut, Almond and
    Raspberry-filled Roll 121
    Raspberry and Hazelnut Yogurt
    Cranachan 55
rice: Kedgeree with Almond Milk 61
    Lamb in Rose-scented Almond
    Sauce 102
    Pumpkin, Chicken and Pumpkin
    Seed Milk Soup 71
    Turkey in a Coconut and Cashew
    Nut Sauce 95
    Tuscan Rice Cake with Almond
    Milk 112
rose water: Almond Milk and Rose
    Water Blancmange 106
    Lamb in Rose-scented Almond
    Sauce 102

salads 80–3
salt 7, 35
Scones: Brown Scones with Oat Milk
    118
Seafood and Cashew Nut Milk Purée
    75

seed and grain milks 30–1
seed butters 48–9
    ways to use 50
seeds: buying and storing 17
    definition 15
Sesame Seed Butters: Sichuan
    Noodles with Sesame Sauce 89
    Tahini 49
    Toasted Sesame Seed Butter 49
sesame seeds 16
    Coconut, Seed and Nut Granola
    with Nut Yogurt 55
    Fruit and Seed Butter Breakfast
    Bars 59
snacks 72–9
soups 64–71
spelt flour: Seeded Nutty Spelt Bread
    with Sunflower Milk 116
spices 35
Sprout Salad with Cashew Nut
    Cream Dressing 82
strawberries, chocolate, coconut and
    Almond Torte 110
sugar 7, 36
Sunflour Milk 30
    Seeded Nutty Spelt Bread with
    Sunflower Milk 116
sunflower seed butter 6, 48
    Fruit and Seed Butter Breakfast
    Bars 59
sunflower seeds 16
    Coconut, Seed and Nut Granola
    with Nut Yogurt 55
    Fruit and Seed Butter Breakfast
    Bars 59
superfood blends 35
sweet potatoes: Pumpkin, Peanut
    and Coconut Milk Curry 84
    Roasted Vegetables with Peanut
    Sauce 85
sweetening milks 36–7

Tahini 49
    Aubergine Dip with Tahini and
    Almond Yogurt 72
    Tahini Hummus 74
Teabread, Peanut Butter 120
terrine: Haddock and Salmon Terrine
    with Cashew Cream 76
tofu: Peanut Butter and Tofu Cutlets
    78
tools and equipment 18–19
turkey: Turkey in a Coconut and
    Cashew Nut Sauce 95
    Turkey with Walnut Sauce 94

unsaturated fats 9

vermouth: Onion Soup with Almond
    Butter and Milk 68
vitamin E 9, 23

walnut butter 50
    Turkey with Walnut Sauce 94
walnut milk 6, 27
    Apple and Walnut Milk Flummery
    107
    Pear, Ginger and Walnut Milk
    Shake 62
Walnut Milk Yogurt: Spicy Walnut
    Yogurt Dip 73
walnuts 15
    Spicy Walnut Yogurt Dip 73

yogurt: Almond Yogurt with
    Pomegranate and Grapefruit 54
    Nut Milk Yogurt 37
    Raspberry and Hazelnut Yogurt
    Cranachan 55

ADDITIONAL NUTRITIONAL INFORMATION

p20 Simple Cashew Nut Milk Energy 507kcal/2122kJ; Protein 0gm; Carbohydrate 23g, of which sugars 23g; Fat 19g, of which saturates 7.0g; Cholesterol 0mg; Calcium 0mg; Fibre 2.3g; Sodium 660mg

p24 Simple Unsweetened Almond Milk Energy 100kcal/419kJ; Protein 3.3g; Carbohydrate 3.6g, of which sugars 0g; Fat 8.3g, of which saturates 0g; Cholesterol 0mg; Calcium 0mg; Fibre 4.4g; Sodium 533mg.

p25 Light Almond Milk Energy 133kcal/558kJ; Protein 3.3g; Carbohydrate 16.7g, of which sugars 16.7g; Fat 6.7g, of which saturates 0g; Cholesterol 0mg; Calcium 0mg; Fibre 0g; Sodium 533mg.

p26 Hazelnut Milk Energy 440kcal/1842kJ; Protein 4.8g; Carbohydrate 52g, of which sugars 25.6g; Fat 22.4g, of which saturates 0g; Cholesterol 0mg; Calcium 0mg; Fibre 0g; Sodium 0mg.

p27 Walnut Milk Energy 546kcal/2285kJ; Protein 12g; Carbohydrate 24g, of which sugars 0g; Fat 48g, of which saturates 6g; Cholesterol 30mg; Calcium 0mg; Fibre 8g; Sodium 363mg.

p27 Pecan Nut Milk Energy 94kcal/392kJ; Protein 3.1g; Carbohydrate 3.4g, of which sugars 0g; Fat 7.8g, of which saturates 0g; Cholesterol 0mg; Calcium 0mg; Fibre 4.2g; Sodium 500mg.

p27 Macadamia Nut Milk Energy 192kcal/804kJ; Protein 2.1g; Carbohydrate 3.7g, of which sugars 1.3g; Fat 20.3g, of which saturates 3.2g; Cholesterol 0mg; Calcium 0mg; Fibre 3g; Sodium 13mg.

p28 Pistachio Milk Energy 349kcal/1451kJ; Protein 11.9g; Carbohydrate 16.1g, of which sugars 4.5g; Fat 26.8g, of which saturates 3.2g; Cholesterol 0mg; Calcium 0mg; Fibre 8.1g; Sodium 11mg.

p28 Brazil Nut Milk Energy 122kcal/512kJ; Protein 2.4g; Carbohydrate 16.8g, of which sugars 15.1g; Fat 7.2g, of which saturates 2.4g; Cholesterol 0mg; Calcium 0mg; Fibre 0g; Sodium 0mg.

p29 Chestnut Milk Energy 208kcal/864kJ; Protein 19.2g; Carbohydrate 4g, of which sugars 1.6g; Fat 12.8g, of which saturates 1.9g; Cholesterol 0mg; Calcium 104mg; Fibre 4g; Sodium 256mg.

p30 Sunflower Seed Milk Energy 300kcal/1256kJ; Protein 10.4g; Carbohydrate 10.3g, of which sugars 1.5g; Fat 26.1g, of which saturates 2.2g; Cholesterol 0mg; Calcium 0mg; Fibre 5.8g; Sodium 15mg.

p30 Pumpkin Seed Milk Energy 71kcal/299kJ; Protein 14.4g; Carbohydrate 0g, of which sugars 0g; Fat 25.6g, of which saturates 0g; Cholesterol 0mg; Calcium 0mg; Fibre 1.6g; Sodium 0mg.

p31 Hemp Seed Milk Energy 501kcal/2090kJ; Protein 23.8g; Carbohydrate 28.5g, of which sugars 24.9g; Fat 33.2g, of which saturates 4.8g; Cholesterol 0mg; Calcium 95mg; Fibre 6.3g; Sodium 0mg.

p31 Oat Milk Energy 412kcal/1727kJ; Protein 1.5g; Carbohydrate 7.5g, of which sugars 36.2g; Fat 9g, of which saturates 0g; Cholesterol 0mg; Calcium 0mg; Fibre 0g; Sodium 0mg.

p33 Whipped Coconut Cream Energy 88kcal/380kJ; Protein 1.2g; Carbohydrate 19.6g, of which sugars 19.6g; Fat 1.2g, of which saturates 0.8g; Cholesterol 0mg; Calcium 116mg; Fibre 0g; Sodium 440mg.

p37 Nut Milk Yogurt Energy 425kcal/1799kJ; Protein 2.8g; Carbohydrate 90.1g, of which sugars 41.1g; Fat 8.4g, of which saturates 0g; Cholesterol 0mg; Calcium 0mg; Fibre 11.2g; Sodium 154mg.

p38 Almond Milk Cheese Energy 464kcal/1943kJ; Protein 65g; Carbohydrate 29.9g, of which sugars 19.5g; Fat 9.3g, of which saturates 0g; Cholesterol 0mg; Calcium 0mg; Fibre 12.4g; Sodium 1764mg.

p40 Smooth Peanut Butter Energy 2732kcal/11313kJ; Protein 102.6g; Carbohydrate 59g, of which sugars 30.1g; Fat 233.1g, of which saturates 57.5g; Cholesterol 0mg; Calcium 166mg; Fibre 0g; Sodium 1575mg.

p42 Crunchy Peanut Butter Energy 2727kcal/ 11300kJ; Protein 112g; Carbohydrate 34.6g, of which sugars 19.8g; Fat 238.9g, of which saturates 42.8g; Cholesterol 0mg; Calcium 212mg; Fibre 36g; Sodium 1665mg.

p43 Almond Butter Energy 2857kcal/11959kJ; Protein 100g; Carbohydrate 92.1g, of which sugars 0g; Fat 257.1g, of which saturates 28.6g; Cholesterol 0mg; Calcium 0mg; Fibre 76.2g; Sodium 0mg.

p43 Almond Chutney Energy 79kcal/330kJ; Protein 3.1g; Carbohydrate 3.4g, of which sugars 1.3g; Fat 6.1g, of which saturates 0.5g; Cholesterol 0mg; Calcium 61mg; Fibre 0.7g; Sodium 201mg.

p44 Cashew Nut Butter Energy 2350kcal/9836kJ; Protein 75g; Carbohydrate 107.5g, of which sugars 0g; Fat 200g, of which saturates 50g; Cholesterol 0mg; Calcium 0mg; Fibre 0g; Sodium 0mg.

p45 Hazelnut Butter Energy 2798kcal/11553kJ; Protein 56.4g; Carbohydrate 24g, of which sugars 16g; Fat 276g, of which saturates 20.8g; Cholesterol 0mg; Calcium 560mg; Fibre 34.7g; Sodium 24mg.

p46 Chocolate Hazelnut Spread Energy 2745kcal/11470kJ; Protein 31g; Carbohydrate 302.5g, of which sugars 298.5g; Fat 165g, of which saturates 46.7g; Cholesterol 10mg; Calcium 650mg; Fibre 5.3g; Sodium 250mg.

p47 Chestnut Butter Energy 511kcal/2166kJ; Protein 5.1g; Carbohydrate 114.4g, of which sugars 40.4g; Fat 6.8g, of which saturates 1.2g; Cholesterol 0mg; Calcium 116mg; Fibre 13.7g; Sodium 31mg.

p47 Coconut Butter Energy 1510kcal/6230kJ; Protein 14g; Carbohydrate 16g, of which sugars 16g; Fat 155g, of which saturates 133.5g; Cholesterol 0mg; Calcium 58mg; Fibre 45.7g; Sodium 70mg.

p48 Sunflower Seed Butter Energy 1688kcal/7063kJ; Protein 56.2g; Carbohydrate 0g, of which sugars 0g; Fat 150g, of which saturates 18.8g; Cholesterol 0mg; Calcium 0mg; Fibre 0g; Sodium 0mg.

p48 Pumpkin Seed Butter Energy 1806kcal/7487kJ; Protein 73.2g; Carbohydrate 45.6g, of which sugars 3.3g; Fat 147.8g, of which saturates 22.6g; Cholesterol 0mg; Calcium 117mg; Fibre 21.2g; Sodium 1036mg.

p49 Tahini Energy 1194kcal/4925kJ; Protein 27.3g; Carbohydrate 1.4g, of which sugars 0.6g; Fat 120g, of which saturates 20.4g; Cholesterol 0mg; Calcium 1005mg; Fibre 15.8g; Sodium 30mg.

p49 Toasted Sesame Seed Butter Energy 1095kcal/4517kJ; Protein 27.3g; Carbohydrate 1.4g, of which sugars 0.6g; Fat 108.9g, of which saturates 18.9g; Cholesterol 0mg; Calcium 1007mg; Fibre 15.8g; Sodium 30mg.

p50 Simple Nut Cream Energy 647kcal/2707kJ; Protein 21.6g; Carbohydrate 0g, of which sugars 0g; Fat 57.5g, of which saturates 7.2g; Cholesterol 0mg; Calcium 0mg; Fibre 0g; Sodium 0mg.

p51 Cashew Nut Cream Energy 967kcal/4046kJ; Protein 26.7g; Carbohydrate 57.3g, of which sugars 0g; Fat 76.7g, of which saturates 0g; Cholesterol 0mg; Calcium 0mg; Fibre 0g; Sodium 433mg.

p51 Dairy Free Pine Nut Pesto Energy 1069kcal/4400kJ; Protein 7.4g; Carbohydrate 3g, of which sugars 2.2g; Fat 114.2g, of which saturates 13.7g; Cholesterol 0mg; Calcium 7mg; Fibre 1.6g; Sodium 1mg.